# THOSE DAYS IN MURAMATSU

# CONTENTS

# FOREWORD (1996)

GRANT K. GOODMAN

> "It's disconcerting that people who behaved so badly in war can behave so admirably in defeat."[1]

Neither any historical document nor any scholarly account has been able to recapture the mood of Japanese-American grassroots interaction in 1945 in the way that Mrs. Yumi Goto does in *Those Days in Muramatsu*. As one who was there in Japan as a member of the American forces in 1945–1946 and as a trained historian of Japan, I feel especially qualified to evaluate the remarkable evocation of an era that Mrs. Goto recounts. Certainly memories dim and memory plays tricks on all of us but since Mrs. Goto recorded her experiences contemporaneously, one feels the profound veracity of her writing. Moreover, the most unusual phenomenon of a Japanese woman purposefully recording her impressions in English so that someday they might be read by Americans reinforces her credibility.

I am particularly pleased to attest to my great personal delight as well as my intense response when Mrs. Goto's work first came to my attention. Indeed, it was her son, Kenichi the distinguished scholar of modern Indonesia and my colleague and friend of many years, was kind enough to share his mother's manuscript with me. In fact, he himself had not known of the existence of *Those Days in Muramatsu* until about ten years ago at the time of Mrs. Goto's

1. Professor B. F. McGuiness quoted in Francis King, *Yesterday Came Suddenly* (London: Constable, 1993), p.90.

having major surgery. According to Prof. Goto, just before his mother, who lives with his family, left for the hospital, she handed him the manuscript and said it was something special to her that she wanted him to have in case she did not survive the operation. Very happily, of course, not only has Mrs. Goto recovered, but her previously unknown manuscript has at last reached publication.

In presenting *Those Days in Muramatsu* to the reading public, it should be remembered that the time frame of it, September to December 1945, was a unique period in the history of Japanese-American relations. Victor and vanquished, occupier and occupied, wartime prosperity and wartime devastation were all immediate attributes of the United States and Japan respectively. In order to appreciate Mrs. Goto's vignettes of that time, psychological factors need to be elicited, in particular euphoria for Americans and despair for Japanese. The Americans who came to Japan, after having defeated both Germany and Japan, were more convinced than ever of the righteousness of democracy American-style while the Japanese, who had been indoctrinated in the superiority of their national "spirituality," in 1945 were in an almost dysfunctional miasma of despond. Curiously, however, at the onset of the Occupation both these attitudes resulted in a high degree of mutual tolerance and generosity. The Americans, missionary-like in their determination to democratize the Japanese, and the Japanese—tabularasa-like in their eagerness to accept *demokurashii*, which, after all, had won the war—found a high degree of common ground, particularly at the human level. And it is at that very human level that Mrs. Goto's insights excite and attract us.

As a member of a distinguished family of educators and as a graduate of the foremost prewar women's college, Tsuda, Mrs. Goto, who had attained a marked fluency in the English language, was, like some others of her generation, well qualified for her role as interpreter between the Occupation and her Japanese employers. As an evacuee from the bombing of Tokyo, it was, of course, pure chance that gave her the unique and surely unanticipated opportunity to work in this capacity in Muramatsu. However, Mrs. Goto was by no means the only educated Japanese woman to utilize her bilingual skills. As one who personally employed at ATIS (Allied Translator and Interpreter Section) at the GHQ SCAP (General Headquarters, Supreme Commander for Allied Powers) tens of such women, some of whom were like Mrs. Goto Tsuda graduates or had studied abroad at such schools as Radcliffe, Wellesley, or Bryn Mawr, I recognize both the contributions these women made to the day-to-day operation of the Occupation as well as to changing the status of women in Japan. For, suddenly, necessity both for desperately needed income for their families and for the requirements of an English-speaking Occupation gave unprecedented opportunities for these women to become breadwinners on an equal footing with their male counterparts. Moreover, at least at GHQ SCAP we were perhaps the first employers in Japan to offer equal pay for equal work. Accordingly, women like Mrs. Goto and her peers were truly pioneers in Japanese society, assuming responsibilities and obligations hithero singularly uncommon among Japanese women.

Further, what Mrs. Goto so tellingly conveys to us in her writing is the almost unbelievable innocence or perhaps insouciance of a bygone era. Her depiction of American GIs as "boys" is so refreshing and so accurate. As one of those "boys," a rosy-cheeked twenty-year-old lieutenant who had grown up in a highly protected, fairly insulated middle-class Midwestern American environment, I recall vividly both my naiveté as I began to occupy Japan as well as my openness to new customs, new insights, new sounds, and most importantly, new ideas. Conversely the Japanese, who had been led to expect their brutalization if not their demise at the hands of us "battle-hardened" enemy soldiers, were charmed and fascinated by everything about us, especially the relative gentility of the Americans whom they encountered.

If all of this is hard to imagine in an era of high tech microchips and hard-nosed Japan-US trade disputes, read Mrs. Goto's revealing account. Of course, 1945 will never come again, but it is, I believe, very valuable to have this meaningful narrative of a simpler and gentler time in the immediate aftermath of such a bloody conflict. Perhaps publishing Mrs. Goto's work now can serve as a valuable reminder to both Americans and Japanese of how we interacted half a century ago. Accordingly, *Those Days in Muramatsu* should generate a certain nostalgia for "the way we were," and, in turn, may serve to mitigate some of the strains in current Japan-US relations.

# PREFACE (1993)

## IN RETROSPECT

YUMI GOTO

For the first time in forty-eight years, I visited the town of Muramatsu last month to refresh my memories. I had heard that the town had a big fire in 1946, but it was virtually an entirely different town from the one I where I spent three months in the fall of 1945 as an interpreter at the railway station.

The streets today are broader with cars passing busily, houses modernized, and no clear rivulet running in the ditch in front of the houses. It is only a small portion of the town that retains the old image with the roof over the sidewalks to provide winter passage through the snow.

When I saw it, I stood still and closed my eyes. Then, the whole scene was revived in my mind. American soldiers in olive drab uniforms, jeeps, trucks, women in kimono, children hailing the passing jeeps with "Goodbye! Hello!"

When I began work as an interpreter, I thought that it was a rare opportunity that not everyone could have, that I would be witnessing the encounter of East and West at a grassroots level, and that, if I wrote a memoir, it would someday become a historical document.

From the beginning, I thought I would write it in English for two reasons. For one thing, I felt that the Japanese people, once the Occupation would be over in the future, would not want to recall the memories of the period when the nation was humiliated but that Americans would like to read about how their young men behaved in Japan. There was the language question, too. I was not familiar with the dialect of the Niigata district and could not reproduce conversations correctly. Moreover, since Japanese personal pronouns are so numerous, I would have great difficulty in choosing which one to use when translating plain "I" and "you" in English.

For all these years, my manuscript mostly slept in my drawer, although I mentioned it to several of my American friends and had copies made for them privately. They all said it must be published, and actually two of them, Mrs. Katie Wenban of Merrimac, Wisconsin and Mr. Peter Thomas of the University of Wisconsin's Public Relations Office, kindly tried unsuccessfully to find a publisher for it.

So I have not touched the manuscript at all, and it contains, I am sure, many awkward expressions and grammatical errors, and there are portions I would write differently if I were to write them now almost half a century later. But I thought I would leave them as they are since they were the thoughts and sentiments of a twenty-six-year-old girl in war-devastated Japan.

During my recent visit to Muramatsu I had a chance to look through the "History of the Town of Muramatsu" compiled by the town office, and I was very gratified to find that it reinforced what I wrote about the American troops in Muramatsu. They were part of the 27th Division and the number of men stationed in Muramatsu totaled 1,843 with the rest of the division stationed in the cities of Niigata, Takada, Sanjo, Kashiwazaki and Shibata in Niigata prefecture. The local history read:

> In the beginning, the townspeople watched with tension how the Occupation troops would behave. But soon they were relieved to find out that they were open-hearted and humane (wartime propaganda said they were "devils and beasts"), and the townspeople quickly reciprocated with goodwill.
>
> The mayor of Muramatsu entertained the American officers at his residence in an effort to encourage personal exchanges, and the US army side sponsored a goodwill basketball match with the towns-

> people at the Muramatsu Elementary School ground. Social and recreational facilities for the American soldiers were provided, and some townspeople were employed at the barracks' kitchen.
>
> The Occupation troops began to go home on December 2, and on December 13, the commander-in-chief of the regiment and the majority of the troops left Gosen on their triumphant trip homeward to New York. On this occasion the regiment expressed its appreciation to the town of Muramatsu for the cordial hospitality given them, and the soldiers waved their hands expressing regret at parting. The remaining team of soldiers all left on December 25.

As I look back on those times, I cannot help thinking how ignorant we were about the world outside and about our own selves. If we had known better, we would have realized that Japan had no chance of winning total war against the Allies. We had no idea until the Nuremberg Tribunal what the Nazis were doing to the Jewish people. Hitler's *Mein Kampf* was widely read in Japan, but we did not know that the paragraphs containing his contemptuous remarks about Japan were omitted from the Japanese translation.

When the coming of US troops to Muramatsu was announced, the townspeople were so depressed and fearful. I was naïve and said, "Why, we are not at war any longer". Perhaps, now I think, men were fearful remembering the atrocities they had seen or heard committed by Japanese soldiers in the conquered lands.

Atrocities are committed in any war, even now, and even among people of the same nation. But the Japanese army was involved in the systematizing of "comfort women" and tortured or killed innocent civilians, to the horror of our hearts.

Furthermore, we even forced the Koreans and Taiwanese to change their names to Japanese ones, and told the people in Asia to worship at the Japanese shrines that the military dared to erect in the occupied areas. It is only in recent years that we in Japan have come to understand how Asian people feel against us.

In comparison, the American soldiers in Muramatsu were simply admirable. It is my great pleasure to have my story available, though the good offices of Professor Grant K. Goodman, to American people who are interested in promoting friendship between two peoples across the Pacific Ocean.

Tokyo, Japan
May 1, 1993

# MAP OF JAPAN

# INTRODUCTION

## DAYS OF AMBIVALENCE IN MURAMATSU

ELIZABETH SCHULTZ

Like other personal writings, Yumi Goto's memoir, *Those Days in Muramatsu,* is both private and public. It reflects upon an interlude not only in her personal history but also in the social history of Japan. More precisely, Mrs. Goto's memoir reflects upon those days from September to December 1945 when she served as an interpreter for the railroad company working with the American military stationed as part of the Allied Occupation in Muramatsu, a small rural town in the province of Niigata in northern Japan. As such, the memoir illuminates a significant moment in the history of Japan-American relations, during which the lives of diverse people in Muramatsu were connected with the lives of 1,500 American GIs.

Having come to Muramatsu from Tokyo with her husband and her two-year-old son in order to escape the devastating effects of the war upon Japan's capital, Mrs. Goto did not, however, escape the war. Her memoir refers to the loss of her family's home to the incendiary bombing and their long-term deprivations of food, including such luxuries as sugar and sake. A student of English at the elite Tokyo women's school, Tsuda College, Mrs. Goto, like all Japanese during the war, was prohibited from using English; her subsequent, succinct description of the war years as "four years of blank" evokes the sense of an intellectual hiatus that was personally calamitous. At various points in her memoir, Mrs. Goto indicates her conviction that the Japanese people were duped during the war by the propaganda of Japanese politicians and militarists;

she acknowledges the disaster of fighting the technically superior American war machine with bamboo spears and falsification of radio reports proclaiming "No damage" when American bombs were destroying Japanese lives and homes; she comes to perceive the government's legitimizing of expansion in order to resolve Japan's growing population demands as a rationalization that might have been resolved by a birth control policy. Regarding the war's end, she speaks for herself, her family, and many other Japanese: "the feeling of relief was far greater than any other emotion. We could now enjoy the beauty of the sky day and night without any fear. No threatening sound of an alarm siren would disturb our sleep."

Despite her awareness of the tragedies of war, a subtext of *Those Days in Muramatsu* establishes Mrs. Goto as "a patriot": "I loved my country." Against the advice of the men in her family, she had purchased national bonds to support the war effort and was dismayed by the Emperor's announcement of defeat on August 15, 1945: "When I ... knew what he was telling us, something hot and cold ran through my body, and I could not stay with the others. I ran upstairs and cried very hard." Early in her memoir, she describes another interpreter, a man wearing dirty clothes and defiling Japanese culture by eating in public, as representing "a defeated nation." Beginning her own work as an interpreter, she explicitly expresses her own determinism to contribute to the shaping of a new Japan. She would not be one of those who might have had "some knowledge of English" but "no pride in being Japanese". "For, though we were misled and defeated, I had not lost faith and hope in my fellow countrymen." Thus Mrs. Goto's memoir reveals her commitment not only to record her personal memories of her three months of intensive and close work with the American military personnel but also to record these memories in such a way as to represent the vitality and complexity of Japanese culture. Writing *Those Days in Muramatsu* in English in 1946—just a year after the end of the war, Mrs. Goto is primarily addressing an American readership. In the course of the memoir she pauses to present capsule lectures on diverse aspects of Japanese culture, such as the difference between Shintoism and Buddhism, the symbolic subtleties of kimono colors, the nuances of the Japanese language, and the complexities of marriage arrangements. Unlike prewar Asian autobiographers writing in English, Mrs. Goto makes no attempt to exoticize Japan; nor is she writing a cultural handbook. By including these explanations, she appears to be concerned strictly with informing her readers that Japan, though defeated, is not humiliated; that Japan, though occupied, retains its integrity.

Although her primary narrative moves beyond national abstractions to reveal the interactions among diverse personalities in the Japanese and American communities in Muramatsu, Mrs. Goto does generalize about national personality traits. Not only is she always conscious of herself as Japanese, but on her first meeting with Americans, she is quick to associate their appearances and their names with specific nationalities. Throughout her text she continues to differentiate among Americans as to their perceived "Mexican," "Italian," or "French" backgrounds. Conscious of the Japanese wartime policy to demonize Americans, she describes the American soldiers as generally good-natured, almost as innocents abroad. However, if she presents her readers with numerous examples of their good humor and generosity, she also makes a point of describing the good humor and generosity of the people of Muramatsu who were assiduous in arranging parties and dinners for the soldiers. She also notes the insensitivity of some Americans to Japanese culture—referring, for example, to Japanese farming techniques as "primitive" or wearing their heavy shoes on the highly polished Japanese floors. Her lengthy description of an American officer's concerns for the Japanese farm boy injured when he had run out in from of his jeep is balanced by her description of her difficulty in obtaining recompense for the elderly woman whose cart had been destroyed by another American jeep.

Her memoir reveals the fledgling attempts of each culture to learn from the other. She calls the sight of Mr. Mitsuno dressed in Western clothes and incongruously singing a Japanese song and dancing a Japanese folk dance for his American guests "funny," yet she recognizes that the American "boys," far from patronizing him, appreciated his effort and joined him by applauding and jitterbugging. Likewise young women, dancing with the Americans in traditional dress, may have tripped on their slippers, but enjoyed themselves thoroughly. Although *Those Days in Muramatsu* affirms that a principal means by which Americans sought access to Japanese culture was reducing it to mere "souvenirs," artifacts which could be packaged and sent home, she also related the soldiers many attempts to learn Japanese. The description of her excitement in teaching Japanese to a group of eager GIs implies that this activity seemed more meaningful to her than a commercial exchange.

Throughout *Those Days in Muramatsu,* Mrs. Goto gives particular attention to the interaction between Japanese women and American men. Although demonstrative of her determination to remain loyal to her country, Mrs. Goto's memoir anticipates dramatic changes in gender relations that events of the war and Occupation accelerated. She exposes her anxiety about changes in Japan's traditional patriarchal system, simultaneously reinforcing this system even as she takes a subversive position against it. Japan's new democratic constitution, outlined in large part by General MacArthur and based on the principles of the Declaration of Independence and the US Constitution, was approved by the Japanese Cabinet in March 1946, and put into law by the Japanese Diet by November 1946, shortly after Mrs. Goto returned to Tokyo from Muramatsu and began writing her memoir. In addition to other liberalizing changes, the new constitution revised the status of Japanese women, giving them for the first time the rights to vote, to own property as individuals separate from their husbands, to succeed to the same share of the family inheritance as their brothers, and to apply for divorce on the same grounds as their husbands. Acknowledging that "It has ... become quite common to attribute to the Occupation, and specifically even to the informal example of the GIs treatment of women, the chief influence for bringing about the change in the status of women in Japan," [1] Kazuo Kawai argues that liberalizing changes in women's lives had been underway in Japanese society before the Occupation. *Those Days in Muramatsu* validates both arguments—the accepted opinion, cited above, assigning the Occupation the revolutionary role in restructuring Japanese women's lives—as well as Kawai's positionstressing a gradual reformation in their lives.

That Mrs. Goto perceived herself to be a liberated woman before the legalization of women's rights in the new postwar constitution is apparent from the first section of her memoir. In the opening lines of the narrative she shows herself to be a conventional wife, expressing hesitancy regarding her husband's and the town's approval of her application for the interpreter's job. However, her dilemma appears immediately resolved as she recalls her antagonism toward the priest of the temple where she and her family first stayed in Muramatsu. She presents him as an archetypical patriarch, tyrannizing over a household of women and an idiot boy and demanding they should address him as "my lord." Her recollection of the priest reprimanding her for reading an English book and lecturing her for two hours to the effect "that knowledge of such a kind was unnecessary for a Japanese woman whose duty it was to do domestic work and take care of her children," results in her decision to assert herself independently. Her recollection of this old man's limited view of women's capabilities, she explicitly tells her readers, leads her to persuade her husband to move out of the temple into a house in Muramatsu, but she also tells them

1. Kazuo Kawai, *Japan's American Interlude* (Chicago and London: U of Chicago Press, 1979) 243–44.

that this recollection—and not her husband's permission—was the catalyst in her decision to use her skills outside of the traditional domestic sphere. Although both she and the Americans left Muramatsu in December 1945, during her brief stay in Muramatsu she proved herself an able interpreter for the Muramatsu railroad and the American military as well as an enthusiastic language teacher. Thus Mrs. Goto's memoir reveals that like many other Japanese women who assumed new work responsibilities in both rural and urban settings, she and Miss Kato, her fellow interpreter, readily met the challenge.[2]

In the second section of *Those Days in Muramatsu,* Mrs. Goto lists seven precautions established by the town's neighborhood organizations to insure their protection from the arriving Americans. Although the list reflects their fear of an enemy bent on pillage and plunder, their final recommendation reflected their fear regarding women. Cautioning women to cover their bodies by wearing *mompe* (loose-fitting trousers, traditionally worn by women engaged in hard labor) and *tabi* (traditional two-toed socks) and not breast-feeding in public, Item #7 obviously was written to

2. Kawai notes that the tendency of industrialization to break up the collective authority of the rural family was "particularly pronounced during the war...when as a result of the manpower shortage women flocked into industry in larger numbers than ever before. Women ran the streetcars and the railway and subway trains, women handled much of the food-rationing, women conducted much of the firefighting activities during the air raids, and women generally took over much of the work formerly considered to be solely the province of men" (244). Elfrieda Berthiaume Shukert and Barbara Smith Scibetta in *War Brides of World War II* (Novato, CA: Presidio Press, 1988) point out that "By April 1946, the first Japanese women were seen policing streets in Tokyo and patrolling railroad stations, once exclusively male occupations" (187). Dorothy Robins-Mowry in *The Hidden Sun: Women of Modern Japan* (Boulder, CO: Westview Press, 1983) writes, "In the unusual years of the 1940s, many capable young women established careers that subsequently took them to top positions in business, public relations, mass media, government, and academia. In the wartime, they had moved diligently ahead because the absence of men had provided rare opportunities. Often a little knowledge of English made all the difference in the boost that the Occupation circumstances offered" (109–10).

discourage American men from finding Japanese women sexually alluring. Word from Tokyo had reached Muramatsu that "young women were moved to the safer mountain side to avoid being raped by the Americans," and several families with whom Mrs. Goto spoke, while expressing their anxiety that the Americans would deprive them of their food, expressed special concern for their daughters' protection. In their study of World War II brides, Elfrieda Berthiaume Shukert and Barbara Smith Scibette quote women from other parts of Japan as remembering, "I was only thirteen years old. Scared. My older girlfriends shaved their heads so they would look like men!" as recalling a mother's warning that "when the American troops arrived, they would rape and murder girls like me and I must hide myself and not let myself be seen." [3] With the actual arrival of the American soldiers, whose faces, in Mrs. Goto's words, showed astonishingly "no hatred, no contempt," the fears of the Muramatsu community were initially dispelled, and in short order this New York regiment and the women from Muramatsu were becoming acquainted. The severity of the restrictions placed on American troops by SCAP (Supreme Commander for the Allied Powers)—rape was punishable by the death penalty, for example—as well as their restraint reduced people's worry over possible sexual aggression; Mrs. Goto explains to an American journalist stationed in Muramatsu the town's attitude toward the GIs: "They like American soldiers because they don't behave like victors. They like you because you are friendly, frank, and good-mannered. No complaint has been heard regarding your behavior. There was one case of a soldier stealing money from a girl with whom he had spent the night, but the soldier was duely (*sic*) punished, the people concerned were satisfied."

*Those Days in Muramatsu* records a diversity of relationships that evolved between American soldiers and Japanese women during the Occupation. Although some women like Mrs. Goto herself and Miss Kato were involved with the Americans profes-

3. Shukert and Scibetta, 185.

herself and Miss Kato were involved with the Americans professionally, as Mrs. Goto's memoir evidences, the sexually charged atmosphere these men generated was both liberating and frightening. Mrs. Goto clearly enjoyed joking with these Americans, and their flirtatious attentions were flattering. When praised for being able to "understand our jokes as well as any American girl," she seems to be asking for approval from her American audience. However, other incidents in her narrative indicate her determination to prevent amiable flirtation from becoming sexual harassment; thus she tactfully puts off the lieutenant who seductively asks her, "Do Japanese people kiss?" and later reproaches him when he picks her up in his arms to lift her out of a Jeep, telling him emphatically, "Don't! This is not a Japanese custom." Miss Kato, derogatorily characterized early in the memoir as "an educated spinster" and represented throughout as being hopelessly infatuated with one of the soldiers, does not protest, however, when he, on the day of the troops' departure from Muramatsu, picks her up and carries her the length of the train to deposit her on the platform outside.

Other relationships between Japanese women and American men demonstrate Mrs. Goto's discomfort regarding the atmosphere of sexual freedom evoked by the Occupation. She describes the soldiers' eagerness to make contact with Japanese women, sitting on railings and whistling "especially at the pretty girls," almost as a parody of male behavior in Western films. If the soldiers sought out families with daughters to visit in the town and organized special parties on the base for them, their presence in the town also led to an increased number of prostitutes in areas around American military bases throughout Japan.[4] To Mrs. Goto's consternation, the soldiers' response to all young women in kimono was to assume they were "Geisha girls! Geisha girls!", synonymous in their minds with prostitutes. Subsequently, however,

4. *See* Spickard, Paul R., *Mixed Blood: Intermarriage and Ethnic Identity in Twentieth-Century America* (Madison: U of Wisconsin Press, 1989) 125.

she hears about "a geisha girl set free by an American soldier," which elicits her exclamation: "It was quite symbolic. The dawn of happy days for the long enslaved women of Japan!" Although she is apparently exuberant at the possibility of change in women's lives, her cliché phrasing suggests a certain irony.

Although *Those Days in Muramatsu* does not document the severe economic conditions of postwar Japan that has been cited as a reason for Japanese women's attraction in such numbers to American soldiers during the Occupation[5], it provides convincing testimony that many Japanese women found new means of self-expression with these young men. With them, they enjoyed dancing, dating, and riding in jeeps in the moonlight for the first time. According to Ijichi Junsei, the Occupation encouraged their developing a "new interpretation and philosophy of love and marriage."[6] In contrast with the liberating possibilities opening up for young women by the Occupation, Mrs. Goto, however, presents the oppressive situation of Mrs. Kuno, the wife of the managing director of the railroad for which she served as interpreter, and of their daughter, Kazuko. Mr. Kuno is described as drinking excessively, maintaining a mistress and a second family, humiliating both his wife and his mistress by forcing a meeting between them, compelling his wife to serve him elaborate meals in solitary splendor, and subjecting her to repeated physical and emotional abuse. Although her husband is directly responsible for arranging Kazuko's divorce, Mrs. Kuno herself cannot obtain a divorce. Mrs. Goto exclaims to her American readers, "Poor Japanese Women! And they dare not sue for divorce. Because, if they are divorced, the old Japanese civil law did not provide for their support from their former husband. Moreover, a divorce is still considered a disgrace and the blame is almost always placed on the woman." In telling the stories of Kazuko and her mother, Mrs. Goto's memoir demonstrates the double bind in which Japan's divorce laws placed

5. Spickard, 126.

6. Quoted in Spickard, 127.

women in: the Kuno women were damned if they did and damned if they didn't. At the end of *Those Days in Muramatsu,* Mrs. Goto's sympathetic description of Kazuko's tearful parting from the American soldier with whom she fell in love suggests that as a result of the Occupation, Kazuko found a means of assuaging the disgrace and blame of her divorce.

In the course of her memoir, however, Mrs. Goto shows her uncertainty regarding the propriety of the relationships between Japanese women and American men. In a section titled "Worried Parents," she devotes four paragraphs to an explanation for her American readers of the complex and careful precautions undertaken by Japanese families in arranging their daughters' marriages. The apparent rationale for such a detailed and lengthy explanation is the necessity of illustrating how an association with an American man could be injurious for a Japanese woman's marriage opportunities. "A girl's reputation is very important," Mrs. Goto concludes. "Sometimes, the young man's family will send someone to ask about [the] girl at her neighboring houses. If neighbors should talk about her as 'She used to go with American soldiers', it might spoil her future happiness. It was quite natural that the girls' parents were not very happy about their daughters going to camp. I could not blame them." Just as she herself had been sensitive to the possibility of negative communal opinion when she stepped outside conventional Japanese gender patterns to apply for her interpreter's job, Mrs. Goto appreciates the concerns of the parents of these young women of marriageable age who had discovered the pleasures of spending time with young men from another culture. A cluster of deeper concerns forms an unspoken rationale behind Mrs. Goto's explicit concern for the young women's reputation and communal opinion, however: Japanese women's exposure to radical ideas regarding independence in marriage, the increase of sexual promiscuity, the loss of racial purity.[7] In addition, her con-

7. American apprehension about interracial marriages is readily documented. Spickard provides evidence that "the occupational authorities encouraged dating, consorting with

sistent reference throughout this discussion of Japanese engagement procedures to the "girl," on the one hand, and the "man" or "young man," on the other hand, indicates her reinforcement of Japanese gender differences. Identifying the women always as "girls," she classifies them in specifically sexual terms, signifying her own and the culture's anxieties for their sexual and experiential immaturity. She perpetuates this constricting gender pattern by further claiming in her discussion that "Girls have always been on the passive side."

Although uncomfortable with either a radical democratic or feminist agenda, Yumi Goto's own actions and assertions in *Those Days in Muramatsu* contradict her conventional descriptions of Japanese women. The act of reflecting on her experience as mediator between the Japanese and the Americans in Muramatsu and of writing a memoir of these experiences in English for American readers suggests the antithesis of passivity; the fact that her manuscript remained unknown and unread suggests not the author's passivity but the lack of attention given in both America and Japan to women's writing, to informal writing such as diaries and memoirs, as well as to the historical importance of the Occupation. Indeed, her entire document is a denunciation of her husband's affectionate, but opprobrious term for her: "silly girl." Ambivalent toward changes in Japanese social and political life especially as it would apply to women, changes which the Occupation was has-

prostitutes, and even informal living arrangements in order to prevent soldiers from taking what they saw as the more drastic step of entering into formal marriages" (132). Public Law 271, passed in December, 1945, and known as "The War Brides Act," was written to assist GIs in Europe but specifically excluded spouses of "racially ineligible races," including the Japanese, who according to the terms of the Exclusion act of 1924 had been so designated. The Occupation Command Report notes that given the prohibition of marriage between military personnel and Japanese nationals, "when applications for marriage to Japanese were submitted, the chaplains could only attempt to persuade the applicant by pointing out the racial, social, and nationalistic difficulties that might arise from such a union" ["Occupational Monograph of the Eighth United States Army in Japan," Vol. III (Sept. 1946–Dec. 1947)] 146. Not until 1952 with the McCarran-Walter Act, did Congress remove racial restrictions on immigration.

tening, Mrs. Goto provides a vibrant record of her feelings and excitement toward them. With its publication, more than fifty years after it was written, her account of *Those Days in Muramatsu* succeeds in giving her readers the opportunity to contemplate America's role in the process of democratizing and feminizing by allowing them to focus on those pivotal days in her life.

# CHAPTER 1

# THE MOUNTAIN TEMPLE

"Head Office Upstairs. The Kambara Railroad Co."

In front of the door that led to the office upstairs I stopped and hesitated a little.

"Is it really all right for me to apply for the job without consulting my husband? What would the town people say?" was my question. I had come down to the station after seeing a newspaper advertisement: "Interpreter wanted at the Muramatsu Station."

While I stood there a scene flashed through my hesitant mind—a scene in the mountain temple where I had stayed about three months before.

After our house in Tokyo was destroyed in an air-raid in January, we—my husband, our two-year-old boy, and myself—went from place to place looking for a house to stay in and finally settled down in an old mountain temple, the priest of which was my deceased father-in-law's acquaintance. The temple was situated in a mountain five miles away from a small town called Muramatsu, and it took us twenty minutes to get there from the nearest house at the foot of the mountain. It was such a secluded place. Not even the alarm siren was heard, and the perfect peace and security were appreciated.

The days I spent there, however, were far from pleasant. There were only five people living besides us in the big, centuries-old temple which could accommodate a few thousand at the time of its annual summer festival.

The temple, surrounded by tall cedar trees and a rapid stream, was dark and humid even during the day and was full of a feudalistic atmosphere. The priest who was called "my lord" was old, sick—half-paralyzed—impatient and ill-tempered. There were two sisters to attend to him. The elder sister Yaye-san had been his maid, and when his wife died, she was adopted as his daughter and had served him ever since. She was proud of it and acted like the queen of the temple. Being thirty-seven, pretty and yet unmarried, ill-tongued villagers who hated the arrogance of the priest and this woman talked behind her back that she was his mistress. Anyway, she did not like my presence because I was the only one she could not order about. The younger sister, Ito-san, I liked and sympathized with. She was of my age and, like her sister, was also unmarried, serving as kitchen maid to her sister and the old priest.

There was another girl, Shige-chan, who was their niece. She was thirteen, big for her age and rather attractive. But she was very lazy and stubborn, and was always disobeying and quarrelling with her aunts because she knew that the old man loved her and would always take her side.

The second male member was a man, a half-wit called Heizo. He was thirty-seven, and had served at the temple for more than twenty years. He was loved and pitied by all the villagers. His only pleasure in life was to eat, eat, and eat. In fact, one of the reasons for the resentment of the village people against the elder sister was that, since she came, Heizo was not allowed to eat as much as he wanted. He was given only three bowls of rice at one meal while he used to eat ten or more. One of the villagers told me that Heizo was half-starving of late.

This temple belonged to the Zen sect of Buddhism, was the oldest and biggest in the prefecture, and, as it was the sacred training ground for the monks, no woman had ever been allowed to live there. However, when the ailing priest's abode in Tokyo was burnt down, the conservative villagers had to give consent reluctantly to the priest's request to take Yaye-san back with him.

There was a special relationship between the temple and the village. There were four families that were called the "folks at the gate" who served as retainers to the temple. Firewood cutting and other labor was offered by the whole village without any payment. The priest and the village master, an almost hereditary position, were the two outstanding figures in the village.

In such a feudalistic atmosphere, I was a misplaced being. People at the temple, with the exception of Heizo, did not like educated women. One day I was called to the room of "my lord" and was severely reprimanded for reading an English book. Yaye-san must have reported it since the old man could not even sit up in his bed. He said that knowledge of such a kind was unnecessary for a Japanese woman whose duty was to do domestic work and take care of her children. During the two hours of his lecturing I remained stubbornly silent, listening to the sound of the stream running under the eave.

This scene flashed through my hesitant mind and gave me courage, "He shall see that a woman can serve her country with such knowledge." My husband who came back from Tokyo where he spent most of his time and was shocked at the change in my look during his absence of one month would understand. I had completely lost my cheerfulness staying at the temple, and he proposed to move down to the town on the following day.

## CHAPTER 2

# THE ANXIOUS INHABITANTS

The town of Muramatsu was located in the middle part of Niigata Prefecture, which is famous for its deep snow and good crop of rice. The population, which originally was only about a few thousand, had increased to over 10,000 since the outbreak of the war, with the growing number of evacuees from big cities. It was a small town with only one broad street that you can explore from one end to the other in less than twenty minutes.

In feudal times it was the site of the residence of the lord, and, as a result, the people of the town were rather quiet and well-mannered compared with the rough-talking inhabitants of the neighboring town, Gosen. Most of the people had never been to a great city like Tokyo and had no idea of what an American was like. An old woman in the neighborhood one day was quite impressed by a picture of a Westerner that she found in my two-year-old boy Ken-chan's picture magazine, and looked at it as long as my boy would let her hold it. "Do they really have such blue eyes and long noses?" was her comment.

So you can well imagine the panic felt by the townspeople when it was announced that American troops were coming to the town to stay at the former Army Signal School that was located in the outskirts of the town.

An emergency meeting was held by every *Tonari-gumi* (neighborhood organization) and under the bright electric lamps that we enjoyed after years of dusky light, such items as the following were read to the anxious men and women of the town:

1. On the day when the troops come in, every shop must close its doors and people must stay inside quietly. Peeping through the window will not be tolerated.

2. During the night keep the outside light bright, lock the doors carefully and stay in the darkened interior.

3. Store your valuable objects away in safe places.

4. When an American soldier comes to your house when you are alone, beat a bucket, basin, or anything that makes noise to notify your neighbors and gather as many people as possible.

5. If a soldier should attack you, try and get something that will identify him later.

6. Tell all the children to behave themselves in order not to invite their anger.

7. *Mompe* (a kind of slacks worn by women during the war) must be worn by all the women all the time. Also wear *tabi* (socks) and do not breast-feed your baby when they are around.

It was about the middle of September. And some people who had recently been to Tokyo came back with the rumor that in Tokyo all the young women were moved to the safer mountain side to avoid being raped by the Americans. I denied the rumor flatly, but later was surprised to find that the family of my husband's aunt who had three daughters and no male member to protect them was actually taken to the country by a Navy truck—one of the daughters was working in the Navy Office—and came back after a week to find most of their valuable furniture stolen by a sneakthief!

Even in Tokyo it was like this. So it was not surprising that when the people gathered at the house of the head of the *Tonari-gumi* they would not move to go home even after the meeting was over.

Under the bright electric lamp they sat with anxious brows and asked one another what to do. Should they send their daughters to their relatives' homes in the village? What would be left for them to eat if 15,000 soldiers came and took all the rice and potatoes away?

I assured them that as the war was over and the Americans were civilized people, they would do no harm to innocent people. Besides, they would not eat rice or vegetables that were raised with night-soil. They were still incredulous, but when the headman told them that the troops coming to their town were a part of the Regiment belonging to the NY Division that was highly praised for its good discipline, they apparently felt more at ease and the meeting ended up with such jokes as, "I think the best way to protect oneself if they should try to kiss you is to bite their projecting nose," and "Don't be silly. No one would even look at such an old woman as you are!"

The people in the village were harder to persuade. A few days later, I went to a nearby village to buy some vegetables at a farmer's house that I had visited several times before. I went into the kitchen as usual. In the dark kitchen, even during summer, they kept a brisk fire all the time, and I would always find the old woman and her grandchildren gathered together by the fireside. But that day I felt a difference. There was no fire, but everybody was there—the grandmother, the farmer, his wife, two sons, and two daughters. They were all silent; no tea cups could be seen. Only dark dejected faces.

"Good morning! Why, is someone ill?" I could not help asking.

"No, no one is ill," the grandmother replied.

"Then what are you so much worried about? Is it a holiday today that you all stay at home instead of working in the rice field?"

"Not that. We don't feel like going to work today, because we've heard that American soldiers are coming to Muramatsu. They will take our daughter, Mitsuko, and make our sons work as slaves. Besides, they will confiscate all our foodstuff, and we shall have to starve and die."

This was the reason why they looked so sad. I felt almost angry at their ignorance. After an hour's chat, however, they seemed to feel less heavy-hearted and, finally, the farmer stood up to get some potatoes for me from the storeroom.

"As you are an educated lady, what you say is probably right, I suppose," the grandmother said and stroked the hair of the five-year-old girl while Mitsuko, the sixteen-year-old attractive girl cast a shy smile of relief in my direction.

Meanwhile, the town officials were busy making preparations for the coming of the troops. It was announced that the 1st and 2nd Battalions and the headquarters of the Regiment were to be quartered at Muramatsu, the total number being about 1,500. The barracks were being repaired, the police station enlarged, and a number of bright electric lamps were newly installed along the streets to assure the people that Americans could not do anything bad even during the night.

I had kept silence as to my having applied for the job. Neighbors would know sooner or later. I found no feeling of resentment against the Americans among the town people. There was only anxiety and curiosity, and I was sure that they would not change their attitude toward me if they knew I became an interpreter. But as my landlord was a wealthy, stingy old man, I was afraid he might turn us out. Anyway, they would find out sooner or later.

## Chapter 3

# THE FIRST AMERICANS IN THE TOWN

It was on a fine warm morning of the 16th of September in 1945 that I first reported to the office of the Kambara Railroad Company. I was introduced to the other interpreter. To my delight, she was a graduate of a college in Tokyo. Miss Kato also came down here as a refugee. She seemed to be a few years older than I was. Very thin and with eyeglasses, she looked exactly what you would imagine from the term "educated spinster". She made friends easily, smoked, and did not hesitate to drink a few cups of *sake* (Japanese wine). Unfortunately for her she had a harsh voice and a terrible giggle that made everybody think, "I wish she would stop that giggling!"

Now, our employer, the Kambara Railroad Company, was a small private company that ran electric trains twice an hour through the plain of the Kambara district. It took just about one hour to go from Gosen, the one end, to Kamo, the other end. Most of the passengers were farmers and their wives and children, whose dialect was hard for me to understand, and boys and girls attending schools in Muramatsu. The landscape along the line was lovely, and, at this time of the year, the range of mountains at the far end of the golden rice fields was quite beautiful against the clear blue sky, which the residents of this prefecture could not enjoy during the five long months of the snow-covered winter.

The head office of the company was on the second floor of the Muramatsu station. As one came up the stairs, the two rooms at the right were those for the president and the managing director, and the big room at the left was the office where several men and women were working. The president of the company was concurrently the mayor of the town—Mr. Machida, about forty-seven, tall and rather good-looking. As Mr. Machida was busy with the affairs of the town, the actual business of the company was run by Mr. Kuno, the managing director. He was between fifty-five and sixty, rather short, liked to talk, especially about himself, and one could tell just by looking at him that he was fond of *sake*. He gave one an impression of being a simple, self-centered and amorous man. He had small eyes that narrowed into mere lines when he smiled after one or two cups of *sake*.

Mr. Kuno introduced us to the people in the office and the station. Then the first work given us to do was to make arm bands for the mayor, manager, and ourselves. "Interpreter"—before we wrote it down with Japanese ink on a white piece of cloth we had to look it up in the dictionary to make sure the spelling was right. It was so long since we had used English—four years!

The train that carried the first American soldiers ever seen in the history of the town was scheduled to arrive at Gosen at one o'clock in the afternoon. So, around noon Mr. Kuno took us to his home, which was a big two-storied house just outside the grounds of the Gosen station. We went in from the back door across the tracks. The house was quite nice. There he lived with his wife, three daughters and a boy who I later learned was the son of the eldest daughter who was divorced from her husband. They were nice and hospitable and we were treated with rice-cakes with lots of sugar on them—that showed how well-off the family was. We had not tasted sugar for ages!

When we came back to the station after a short while, there was a crowd of men and women and boys and girls gathered outside the station wicket. On the platform were the "big shots" of the town: the mayor, police chief, station master and some influential businessmen. They were nervous, too. We knew we were the object of the crowd's curious eyes and we were afraid that we might have forgotten English after four years of inactivity.

"Fifteen more minutes." The station master said looking at his watch.

"The train has just left the Ogarashi station," a man came out of the office and reported.

"Five more minutes..."

At last, around the corner it appeared, puffing black smoke and gradually approaching.

With growing tension, we waited. A hundred meters, fifty meters, ten, five... here it comes. The locomotive passed, and, bump, right in front of us stopped a box-car with its doors open, and out jumped three khaki-clad young men with blue eyes and blond hair.

We drew nearer to them in a silent semi-circle. There was an awkward silence. Someone—newspaper man, probably—poked at me from behind and asked me to inquire their name, rank, age, and who the commander was.

Feeling relieved, I said, "How do you do. Will you please tell us your name, rank, age, and who the commander is?"

With a look of surprise and delight the three young boys started to speak at the same time, "We are..." The one who appeared to be the oldest continued.

"I am Charles Johnson, corporal, twenty-five. These are Richard Grey, nineteen, and Allan Howard, eighteen. Both of them are PFC."

"Who is the commander?"

"Colonel Frost."

"But, he isn't here with you, is he?"

"No. We've lost light of him at Sanjo," and the three chuckled. There must be some mystery.

"Then, which one of you is in charge?"

"I am supposed to be," Johnson replied.

I translated the conversation into Japanese. When the newspaper man asked me in Japanese, "Should it be spelled … or … ?" Mr. Johnson guessing right, pronounced his name clearly again,

"This boy must be smart," I said to Miss Kato.

"When the interview was over, the circle loosened and the boys were free to talk to Miss Kato and me.

"Where did you learn your English?" was their first and unanimous query.

"Have you ever been in the States?"

"We learned our English in Tokyo."

"You speak very good English."

"This is the first time I heard good English spoken since we came to Japan," Grey said offering me a piece of chewing-gum.

"Is this Muramatsu?"

"No, it is the next station. We change here at Gosen."

***The three RTO boys***
***Seated (L to R):*** *Mr. Kuno, Private Howard, Private Grey, Sgt. Johnson, Mr. Machida (President of Kambara Railroad)*
***Standing (L to R):*** *Miss Kato (2nd from Left), Mrs. Goto (3rd from Right), Mr. Mitsuno*

While we were talking, the youngest boy, Howard, began to pace up and down the platform stretching his arms upward and then sideways. They were completely at ease. No self-consciousness of being stared at by more than a hundred people was seen in their attitude. No fear of being among strangers who were their enemies but a month ago. No hatred, no contempt, was found upon their faces. They were as natural and unpretentious as they could be.

Suddenly, a man—a Japanese—popped out of the box-car. He was in wrinkled shirt and wore dirty *geta* (Japanese footgear). And he was eating something and had a piece of cookie in his hand. I felt uncomfortable and ashamed. I felt I saw a defeated nation in him. I learned that he was an interpreter from Yokohama. From now on, perhaps, this kind of man would act important—these men with some knowledge of English but no pride in being Japanese. I was sad. For, though we were misled and defeated, I had not lost faith and hope in my fellow countrymen.

At the same time I wondered why it was that we feel it perfectly natural when we see an American eating something on the street, while we feel contemptuous toward a Japanese adult, be it man or woman, if we see him with his mouth full in the street. Why? Perhaps it is because we are not used to it, but this is a question I cannot solve as yet.

Meantime, the box-cars that were loaded with army stuff were switched over from the government railroad track to the Kambara line, and we all got into the train for Muramatsu.

The three boys' house, that is, the box-car, was pulled up to this end of track No. 1 at the Muramatsu station and we went down to make a social call on them. The car was clean and tidy; three cots, a water container, some boxes, and shirts hanging on hangers. The ordinarily dirty box-car was transformed into a cozy little living room.

An electric light and heater were installed in the car and so the first day of the RTO at the Muramatsu station began.

# CHAPTER 4

## SHOPPING

Miss Kato and I went down to say good night to them before going home.

They were sitting in the car looking rather bored. When they saw us ready to go home, they asked if they might accompany us. They wanted to have a walk and do some shopping.

"With pleasure," we said and set out together.

Now the station was at the far end of the town and a broad road ran through the town. At about half way it branched off into the other big road leading to the main gate of the barracks. It was a good paved road, and two months before we saw students of the Army Signal School marching along it almost every day, perspiring, covered with dust, and singing military songs. Poor boys!

We walked leisurely. People of the town stared at us. Children followed, keeping a cautious distance. The three American boys, in their turn, looked around with curiosity at the roofed sidewalks—in winter when snow falls so heavily and reaches the second floor, this roofed sidewalk becomes a tunnel for people to walk in—at the stones placed on the roof—because of the heavy snow, the roof was made with light boards and the stones were to prevent them from being blown away by the wind—and at women in *mompe* with their babies on their back.

We looked into each and every shop. There weren't many. When we came to a shop that sold miscellaneous goods, Johnson spotted a small mirror on the shelf and went in to buy it. The boys bought mirrors.

"What are you going to do with it?" I asked.

"Just a souvenir," was their answer.

The mirror Johnson picked up had a red back. He held it before him and bashfully said, "Monkey." Indeed, if any one should ask which animal he resembled I should say without hesitation "monkey," and he knew it. However, it was a fine face, grave and trustworthy—German type, to which young Howard also belonged. Grey was obviously of French origin.

We passed the big mayor's house, post office, bank, and, in front of the barber's they said, "I'm coming back here to have a haircut."

At the end of the street, we parted. I assured them that they could not possibly get lost, the town being so small.

Walking toward home together, Miss Kato and I said to each other, "It is very thoughtful of the Americans to send such boys first. They will surely give a good impression to the people of the town."

As we predicted, the "three soldiers at the station" became very popular with the townspeople. Especially Johnson, who remained at the station until the last, who became the best known and most popular of all the American soldiers stationed at Muramatsu.

## Chapter 5

# THE OPENING OF RTO

The next day was a leisurely one. Once, in the afternoon, we went up to Gosen to check a few freight cars, when we met Col. Frost and his interpreter Sgt. Nishi, a Nisei boy. Col. Frost impressed us as having a Slavic face. He was a Lt. Col. but was only twenty-nine. We were told that he was a regular West Point man. He looked older for his age with cropped hair and sleepy-looking eyes. Later we learned that he was rather popular among the men of the regiment, while the commander, Col. Bayne, was much hated and had many nicknames such as "moon-faced Bull Dog," etc.

While we were at the Gosen station, we were invited to have tea with the station master. He was a middle-aged man, round-faced, jocular, and good-natured, and we soon became good friends.

Through our interpreting, he put various questions to the three soldiers and told them to come in and have tea with him whenever they came to the Gosen station.

"Gosen, Station Master!" pointing to his nose he said, pleased with the first English words he ever uttered before the Westerners. He was a good station master. He liked to keep his station clean and tidy, and was particular about cleaning up. And the atmosphere of the station was cheerful and pleasing to the travellers.

This was the first of our innumerable trips between Muramatsu and Gosen. Our job was to receive and ship cargos that were addressed to the Regiment, 1st and 2nd Battalions. At least once every day, sometimes twice, even three times, we went up to Gosen to meet and check the freight cars.

Late that night, my landlord was awakened by the banging at the front gate. It was a messenger from the station requesting me to come to the station at once.

I bicycled to the station—cycling was the only thing I learned while staying at the temple—and went with the three boys to Gosen to meet some soldiers who came on a freight train. They were a captain and some men belonging to the 3rd Battalion stationed at Shibata City. They were to stay overnight at Muramatsu.

I came back home at midnight, sleepy and tired, saying to myself that if this should happen every night, I was going to quit.

# CHAPTER 6

# THE ARRIVAL OF THE TROOPS

The whole town was in a state of silent excitement. This was the day when the troops were coming. They were expected to arrive in the afternoon, and the people were anxious.

We were waiting at the Gosen station, but, as we had regained confidence in our English, we felt less nervous and more composed. I would never be scared by the number of soldiers; I was determined.

About 750 men were to arrive on the first train that was due at one o'clock. At long last it pulled into the station. At first there was no stirring among the passengers. Then a few men got out of the first carriage. It was Col. Payne and his staff, who got into a jeep waiting at the wicket—I did not notice it till then—and went away. Yet, there was no movement in the train. Soldiers were sitting still, with some fellows fast asleep.

A few soldiers noticed me, got up and opened the window.

"This is the station where you get down," I told them, "Please tell the others to get ready".

"Oh, she speaks English!" a soldier remarked.

"What is she? What? In-ter-preter, Interpreter. Good!"

"Hello!"

"Hey! Is this Muramatsu?"

I was showered with questions. But I had no time to answer them all. I went from one carriage to the next telling the soldiers to get ready. In olive-colored uniform and helmets, they all looked alike. I couldn't tell officers from men, so, I just told whomever was nearest to go across the tracks to the far end of the station where the train for Muramatsu was waiting.

In a minute or two, the platform was swarming with soldiers. They all had big bags; some of them carried them on their shoulders, and some dragged them along.

Mr. Kuno, Miss Kato and I got on one of the carriages. Everybody seemed to be talking now. Some were singing. They all looked happy knowing they were nearing the end of their long journey.

"How long does it take to where we get off?" A soldier approached us and asked.

"It's only about seven minutes."

"Is the barracks far from the station?"

"No. About twenty minutes. A nice walk."

While we were engaged in talking, we were already in Muramatsu.

"Here we are!"

And again, they turned into a silent mass of olive-colored uniforms.

In front of the station, they formed lines and with "Tention!" "Forward, March. Hup, two…", which sounded novel to my ears, they marched away, platoon after platoon, towards the barracks.

When I went upstairs to the president's room, I found some officers and interpreters having tea in the room. Among them was a Lt. Grotious. He did not impress me very deeply just then, but he later became my good friend and pal.

## Chapter 7

# CELEBRATION

The second half of the soldiers having safely gone to the barracks, the memorable day for the Kambara Railroad Company ended without any mishap. Mr. Kuno was all smiles, and suggested that we have a party to celebrate the occasion. That was just the thing we wanted. A messenger was sent to the only western-style restaurant in the town, and Messrs. Johnson, Grey, and Howard were cordially invited to come upstairs at six o'clock.

A cloth-covered table was set in the president's room and seven chairs placed around it. There was another table in the adjoining room with the sliding doors between the two rooms thrown open. That table was for the girls working in the office.

At six o'clock sharp the three boys appeared. Clean-shaven and in pressed uniform they looked very happy, and were using all the Japanese words they had picked up.

On the table were flowers. We sat at the table: Mr. Kuno, Mr. Mitsui, Miss Kato and myself beside the boys. Now, Mr. Mitsuno was Mr. Kuno's assistant. He was a short man. Short even for a Japanese. He had his hair cropped short in a way that shopkeepers always do. The girls later told me that he was a hypocrite and that he acted as a spy for Mr. Kuno.

It was a dinner with full course. The three boys ate and drank with relish saying that it was the first real dinner they had since they were drafted. Neither Mr. Kuno nor Mr. Mitsuno was satisfied with being beaten in drinking.

The number of bottles on the table increased as time passed.

I said to Howard who was shouting songs, "You are just a kid. You mustn't drink so much."

"Oh, it's all right. I am a soldier. Besides, whenever I look at a bottle, it looks back at me. So, I can't help drinking it."

Even before I translated, everybody already started laughing. The way he said it was so funny. Little Miss Kaneko who was fourteen and a merry messenger girl was rolling with laughter.

Everybody became merry and more talkative. Johnson was talking to me without paying any attention to the others. He told me that he fell in love with a thirteen-year-old girl when he was fifteen and got married; but after a while, they couldn't get along well with each other and got divorced. Then he married for the second time and had a baby, who was three years old now, and he produced a picture of a girl and her mother and showed it to me. It was a picture of his wife and his daughter.

"She is a beautiful girl."

When I said so, he looked very sad.

"She was. But she was killed in a motor accident."

He then enlisted and was sent over to Germany, where he was captured and was a prisoner. One day, he and his brother, who also had been captured at the same time, and fourteen others broke out of the prison and ran away. However, the attempt failed, and only he and one other fellow could escape. His brother was shot and killed.

He had had enough points to go home, but he had been mistaken for some other Johnson and had been sent here. He said he didn't regret it very much, because he had no wife to come home to and his daughter was being well taken care of by his mother.

Grey said that he was a mechanic and was working in an automobile factory. He had been married only two months when he was drafted, and he was looking forward to going home.

I was surprised to know that both of them were married so young. Howard, the kid, was not much interested in such domestic talk, and was singing one song after another.

Suddenly, Mr. Kuno caught my sleeve and whispered, "Tell them I have a mistress in this town. I want them to know that I am a man of the world and have tasted the sweets and bitters of life."

I had heard that he had a second home in Muramatsu and had two children by his mistress, but to know that he was rather proud of it surprised me. I whispered back a little embarrassed.

"In America it is not considered a good topic to talk about when ladies are around."

"My name is Mitsuno, Honey" (*mitsu* means honey). Mr. Mitsuno was explaining to the boys. "I shall sing a Japanese song."

He stood up, and singing, danced a Japanese folk dance. It was funny as he was in western clothes, but the American boys applauded heartily, and Johnson and Grey stood up to dance Jitterbug, which we enjoyed very much.

When the time came for us to go home, the three boys thanked us again and again for a most enjoyable evening. To which Mr. Kuno replied, "I shall take you to my house in this town some day."

## CHAPTER 8

# GETTING TO KNOW EACH OTHER

What surprised the people and delighted the children of the town the next day was a number of jeeps and big army trucks that suddenly appeared from nowhere during the night.

Whenever a truck or a jeep passed, children forgot that they were told to stay in quietly. They would run into the street, wave their hands and shout at the top of their voice, "Good-bye, Good-bye!" It was a few days afterward that they learned to say "Good-bye! Hello!"

The trucks were busily running back and forth between the station and the barracks carrying boxes and boxes of rations and what not.

Thus, the busy days began for us interpreters. We stood in the yard all day long, interpreting orders for the station people.

"Put that box-car No. 505 on this track, and when the unloading is through, sent it back to Shibata."

"Move that car over there a little forward so that the truck can go through the cars to the box-car on the other end."

"Switch that car over to this side." And so on and so forth.

The station people were smart enough to understand the soldiers by their signs in a day or two. But on the first day, they depended entirely upon our interpreting. For instance, when Johnson motioned the engine to move away, the driver drove it nearer instead, the sign being quite opposite to that of the Japanese. There were some misunderstandings of that sort, of course, but on the whole everything went on smoothly, and people cooperated eagerly.

It was a bright day. The sun was shining and made us quite warm.

"Let's take a break," Grey suggested and we sat down on one of the logs that were piled up in the yard.

There were some other soldiers from the barracks to help with the loading and unloading. One of them who introduced himself as a radio man came to sit by us. He was a slender boy with remarkably beautiful eyes. Our conversation started as usual with "Where did you learn your English?", and he told me about his experiences on the stage in New York.

When his truck was ready to go, he reluctantly got up with, "So long! See you again."

I thought I should never forget this Mr. Tiezin and his most beautiful eyes, but when next time we met on the street, I disappointed him by flatly telling that I did not remember him. But he was to blame for that; he had his sunglasses on that day. At any rate, he had the most beautiful blue eyes I had ever seen. And so innocent looking!

What made me happy while watching the soldiers and the Japanese workers was that the soldiers treated them quite nicely. Some were offering their cigarettes to those workers. They were farmers and people of the town requisitioned. They would go home and tell the folks what they had experienced, thus putting an end to groundless rumors and fears of the Americans, I was sure.

People in the town had already begun to show their interest in the soldiers. When I was home on Sundays, neighbors came to me to ask about the soldiers. Soldiers came in that quiet neighborhood where I lived, and some of the neighbors invited them to come in.

"Two of them came in the other day," a neighbor told me. "They made a gesture of drinking and asked for *sake*. I said 'No, no!' Then, they gave my little daughter a piece of candy and went away. It would be very interesting if I could speak English like you do. I was sorry because all I could say was 'No, no'. If I had any *sake*, I would be very glad to treat them with *sake*, but we have had no ration for a long time, you know." She really looked sorry to have refused them.

Even my landlord, I was glad to know, was quite interested in what I was doing. Squatting by the fireplace in the center of the room, this eighty-year-old man would listen to me with "Is that so!" and "Well, I declare!" And he did not get too mad even when my little boy took his *geta* and sent them floating down the small brook that ran in front of the house.

By and by, the inhabitants of this small northern town began to taste some things that they had never before tasted: American cigarettes and candies. Soldiers were selling them. No one could blame them for it. For they wanted money to buy souvenirs with, but, as they had been transferred from place to place so often, their pay could not catch up with them. They were really in need of pocket money, Johnson told me.

Meantime, Johnson, Grey, and Howard were enjoying their job very much. For one thing, they were free. They did not need any pass when going out. Provided that one of them stayed at the station, they could go out whenever and wherever they wanted. Drinks were abundant. Mr. Kuno and Mr. Machida, the president and mayor, always supplied them with beer and *sake*. Besides, there were many pretty girls at the station to play with or practise conversation with.

"I wouldn't mind staying in the army forever, if it's always like this," was their frank opinion.

## CHAPTER 9

# THE FIRST RIDE IN THE JEEP

I recall it was only a day or two after the arrival of the troops. When I was in the station yard as usual, one of the girls called from the second floor window and said that Mr. Kuno wanted me to come as soon as possible because there was an officer in his room. Leaving Miss Kato in the yard I went up immediately and met a 2nd Lt. called Alan Garden, who afterwards became another of my good friends.

He was a tall man, thin, and reminded me of an eagle. He said he belonged to the regimental headquarters and was in charge of recreation. Today he came to ask Mr. Kuno to show him where the skiing range was. I was thrilled to think that I could have a ride in that cute little vehicle, which they called a "bug".

Mr. Kuno fetched his hat and we climbed on to the jeep. Lt. Garden sat in the front seat. Mr. Kuno, myself, and the Lieutenant's 1st Sgt. sat behind.

It was a beautiful day. The sky was so blue and the mountains and trees so green.

Lt. Garden was always turning back to talk to us.

"I could love you for this lovely trip," the sergeant said to the lieutenant, who laughed heartily, showing his clean white teeth. It was his laughter that attracted me. It sounded so natural and pleasant.

We passed a village or two and after crossing a railroad track, we came into a valley where we could see smooth hills on the left side. "That is the place where we ski."

Mr. Kuno said I translated it faithfully. Perhaps it was because he did not say, "That is the skiing range," but anyhow, after a short while, Lt. Garden turned and asked, "Do we still have a long way to go?"

"Why! The hill that we passed a few minutes ago is the place."

"Then, where are we going now?"

"I don't know. Do You?"

At my pert answer he again laughed, his voice resounding like ripples in the water.

"Now, to the station," he ordered the driver, and we came back slowly enjoying the landscape. It was really a very nice trip. "I could love you for this lovely ride," we could have said, too.

# CHAPTER 10

# LT. FEROCIOUS "BUDOSHU" GROTIOUS

---

"Hello, Sweetness! Have you had your *budoshu* yet today?"

Such was the greeting Lt. Grotious gave me every day.

Lt. Hank Grotious was a very young second lieutenant. He was twenty-three, and the second youngest officer at the camp. As he belonged to S4, he came to the station every day on some business or other. I suspected that he came to have a sip of Mr. Kuno's *sake* even if he had no business at the station, and he told me that my guess was right. "Besides, I come to see you. You mustn't forget that." Although he was younger than I was, he talked as if he were older and was always teasing me when I was not teasing him.

He was also tall and thin with young-boyish blue eyes that brightened up whenever he was planning to tease someone. He was not particularly good-looking. He had a comic pug nose and his hair was of mixed color—a golden streak in chestnut. I did not notice it until one day he picked up some hair and said, "How do you like my hair?"'

"What do you mean?"

"It's of mixed color, you see."

"Oh, I took it for a sign of craziness."

He made a long face.

He was Mr. Kuno's favorite officer. Mr. Kuno always kept a

bottle for "Budoshu-san." He had a hard time trying to remember American names, and he gave up his efforts at last and began to call him "Budoshu-san" which meant grape wine and was an association of thought easy for him to remember.

Lt. Grotious was popular with everybody. He was the most popular officer at the camp, though his nickname was "Ferocious," the three boys told me.

***Frequent visitors to the station office***
***Seated (L to R):*** *Mr. Machida, Lt. Ferocious Grotious, Lt. Marlor, Lt. Sayer, Mr. Kuno*
***Standing (1st Row L to R):*** *Mrs. Goto (in kimono), Miss Kato (3rd from right), Mr. Mitsuono (far right)*
***Standing (2nd Row L to R):*** *the station master (behind Mrs. Goto), Miss Kaneko*

"I like him because he treats us like friends," Grey said. "The other day he caught me when my coat was unbuttoned. He said, 'Button it up, and you will be Mr. Grey.' Other officers would have just thundered at me".

"I like to see him in state too," Johnson said. I agreed. He had a kind of commanding air about him that became him very well.

I often found him in the three boys' room, drinking and joking like good friends. He was smart, too. He picked up simple Japanese words faster than anyone else.

"*Konnichi-wa*," he would say peeping into the head office before going to Mr. Kuno's and, "Kaneko-san, (*san* means Mr., Mrs. or Miss) *o-cha dozo* (tea, please)".

At that, Kaneko-san, the youngest little girl who was always smiling, laughed delightedly and followed Grotious-san with cups of tea on a tray.

"*Oishii* (delicious), *arigato* (thank you). *Mata dozo* (again please)."

Then, he would settle down to a glass of *budoshu* with Mr. Kuno.

As I said before, Lt. Grotious did not make any strong impression on me when we first met, and it was after an afternoon spent together at Mr. Kuno's that we became great pals.

Mr. Kuno, who took a fancy to Lt. "Budoshu", invited him to his home a few days after the troops came in. Lt. Grotious asked if he might take his friend with him, and brought the youngest officer in the regiment, twenty-two-year-old Lt. Hyder.

While we were waiting for the jeep, Mr. Mitsuno came in. He was tipsy and persistently talked to us in his broken, badly-pronounced high school English, bowing incessantly. Lt. Grotious, with his boyish-looking blue eyes filled with merriment, was looking at him for a while, when he suddenly turned toward me and told an account of a monkey which the soldiers had brought back from Okinawa, "We gave him some wine the other day. He got drunk and it was such fun."

He imitated the gestures of the drunken monkey and as it was so good, we laughed and laughed until tears rolled down my cheeks.

"Monkey, Mitsuno-san, *yopparai* (drunkard)," he said triumphantly pointing to Mr. Mitsuno's puzzled face.

Both Lt. Grotious and Lt. Hyder were much surprised and pleased with the hospitality and good dinner served at Mr. Kuno's.

Especially, Grotious-san was in his best humour, displaying all his vocabulary of Japanese.

"*Ojo-san* (young lady) *kirei* (pretty). *Okusan* (Mrs.), *tabako dozo* (please take a cigarette). *Sake oiishii* (delicious)."

They stretched out their long legs, encircling the small Japanese style table, which was placed in front of each guest.

Lt. Hyder, who at first glance seemed a serious kind of man, disclosed his real temperament after a glass or two and was joking and talking like Grotious-san. They started to boast about their respective home towns.

"My town is the best town in the United States."

"It's impossible. Mine is the best."

Lt. Grotious took out pictures of his girlfriend.

"How pretty!" The Kuno girls admired.

"Bah!" Lt. Hyder waved it aside as if disgusted.

In the alcove of the room there were several Japanese swords being displayed. Mr. Kuno explained that he was having a last look at them because he had to turn them in a few days. They were much impressed with the beauty of the swords, and also of the lacquer ware that Mr. Kuno brought out to show them. I later learned that Mr. Kuno's collection of art objects was well-known in the town. Mr. Kuno also showed them a scroll of writing of Admiral Togo, who, contrary to our expectation, was little known to them. However, they had heard about the forty-seven *ronin,* and looked at the letter written by one of them with great interest.

"We have heard that Japanese are hospitable people, but we could not believe it until today. We are really glad we came", they said to Mr. and Mrs. Kuno.

Lt. Grotious said to me, "Talking with you is just like talking with an American girl. Nobody back home will believe me if I tell them that I've met a Japanese girl who could understand our jokes as well as any American girl."

At any rate, Lt. Grotious was a great comedian and at his funny gestures, Mr. and Mrs. Kuno and their three daughters were laughing from the beginning to the end of the evening. It really was a most enjoyable party.

# Chapter 11

## A Shady Deal

Two days afterward, Lt. Grotious came upstairs with his loud "Goto-san!"—he had a voice, though not beautiful, and difficult to describe, which could not be forgotten easily. He thanked Mr. Kuno again for the party and said.

"Hyder must have seen those beautiful lacquer wares in his dream last night. He said, 'Beautiful, beautiful, beautiful!' three times while sound asleep."

Then he pulled me aside and said, "Tell Mr. Kuno I've come to see him about his swords. When I went back to the camp, I asked if there was any way of preventing their being turned in, because they are so beautiful. But no one can disobey General MacArthur's orders. So, if Mr. Kuno likes, I will keep some of his best swords in my room at the barracks and return them to him after a month or two when it's all over."

Naturally, Mr. Kuno was very grateful.

The sooner the better. We all got in his jeep and hurried to Mr. Kuno's. Grotious said that he was particularly interested in the swords because his father too was interested in collecting swords. When Mr. Kuno told him that he would give him a black sheathed one as a gift, he was much delighted.

"This is a shady deal. You mustn't tell anybody," he said and took precaution to hide his shoes when we got to Mr. Kuno's and took off our shoes. We got out of the jeep at the station, not at the gate of the house.

Mr. Kuno selected three of his best swords from his some twenty swords. All of them were several hundred years old and Lt. Grotious was charmed with their beauty. Both parties were quite satisfied with this shady deal.

# CHAPTER 12

# A TRIP TO SHIBATA

One day, at about one o'clock in the afternoon, Lt. Garden came up to the office.

"Goto-san!"

He looked around in the office. I had had my desk moved to a corner near the door, so he did not see me.

"Where is Goto-san?"

"Hello, Lt. Garden."

I rose from under his feet, "You are too tall to notice me."

He asked me to accompany him to Shibata City where the rest of the regiment was stationed. It was about a three-hour ride by train. Mr. Kuno was reluctant to let me go.

"It is too late to start now. You won't be able to get back home until after dark," he said. I knew he thought, "There are some interpreters at the camp. Why must he come to take one of my interpreters?"

Lt. Garden came straight to me, without first paying attention to Mr. Kuno, who, therefore, was not pleased.

However, I knew how fast a jeep was, and it was such a fine day with no freight cars coming in. I didn't mind going out.

When I went down I was disappointed, because the company did not include that sergeant who went with us on the trip to the skiing range. This time it was a boy who reminded me of George Raft, a movie actor, and I didn't like him at all.

We drove fast, crossed the river, and passed many towns and villages where children ran after us and shouted "Hello! Goodbye!" enthusiastically waving their hands. Lt. Garden waved back each time.

The George Raft, whose Italian name I cannot remember, was casting a side glance at me several times, before he slowly moved his foot and stepped on my shoe. I turned and looked straight into his eyes with a look that made him behave himself the rest of the way.

Lt. Garden had a perfect map, but we stopped our jeep a dozen times and asked the way to Shibata. Once I showed them one of my weak points—lack of a sense of direction.

At a quiet village we stopped our jeep at the village office and asked the people there. They took out a map and explained to us minutely. But when we came out of the office, I said to the driver, "To the right." Lt. Garden looked dubiously at me, but said nothing until after five minutes when I realized that we should have gone to the left.

"I thought so," Lt. Garden laughed. "Never mind. I didn't ask you to come as a guide."

I did not mind being looked at by soldiers while Lt. Garden was having a talk inside at the camp. However, what made me very uncomfortable was the staring of the city people, especially women—who just glared at me seeing me in the jeep. I looked back at them haughtily. I wasn't doing anything wrong, I meant to communicate to them. They were mostly women. Men didn't have such intense enmity in their eyes. By the time we left the city, I was feeling very disagreeable and insisted on being back at the station by four.

Lt. Garden seemed to be desirous of a longer ride, but at my childish stubbornness he said, "OK, OK," and ordered the driver homeward.

I could not resist, however, when he said he wanted to stop at Lake Tennoji to see whether the soldiers could come to enjoy swimming and boating. We went to the custodian's house situated by the private lake, and were entertained most cordially. He was a very polite middle-aged man, and he invited us to come back again to enjoy boating. He told Lt. Garden that if he took his gun with him, he could enjoy duck hunting. At this, Lt. Garden was overjoyed, for he was a great lover of hunting.

"A way up in the mountain—"

All the way back home, Lt. Garden was telling me about his hunting trips near his hometown and the game he got.

"I shot a deer, and we kept the meat in the ice-box. It lasted us the whole winter...."

His father was a doctor in Los Angeles. Lt. Garden himself was twenty-six, married, and had a three-year-old girl. He had worked on the improvement of the B-29s before he was sent abroad.

I enjoyed his talking and when we got back to the station, I agreed to going back again to visit Lake Tennoji.

People at the station were much surprised to see me back so soon.

"Did you really go to Shibata?" they asked.

"I wanted to come back soon, because I knew they were worried that you were going to kidnap me," I said to the lieutenant, who got in the jeep laughing.

# CHAPTER 13

## HOUSING PROBLEM AND MR. KUNO

I was talking with Miss Kato one day. Miss Kato, with her mother and two younger sisters, was living with her relatives in a neighboring village. It seemed they were not getting along very well. The relatives were stingy, as is perhaps natural in times of want, and, although they had enough foodstuff to spare, they would not give them to Miss Kato and she had to buy them at high prices from other farmers.

"It is hard to live with these country people. They are fond of giving presents to us, but when they do, they always expect to receive something in return that is better than what they have given. After all, we city people cannot get along well with country people," she said.

She was desperately looking for a house or room in the town. So was I. I wasn't on bad terms with my landlord. Although the old man was rich and miserly, he was willing to give me some of his vegetables if I paid a reasonable price. And his daughter was quite nice to me and she sometimes sold me the old man's rice or beans when he was out. However, his son was coming back from the south now that the war was over and he asked me to move out. It was understood from the beginning, and I could not complain.

I spoke of my situation to Mr. Kuno, who instantly said, "Then come to my house. We have two rooms upstairs that we can rent you. Then I shall always have an interpreter when someone calls upon me, and both of us will profit by it."

I was very grateful and told my husband who came back from Tokyo about it. He was not particularly glad as he didn't want to impose on others' kindness, but, as we had not found a living place in Tokyo, we accepted his offer for the time being.

It was in the beginning of October that we moved to his house. It was a nice house and was always kept clean, because they did not burn wood in the house as almost all other families did. They used charcoal abundantly.

His wife and three daughters were very kind to us and loved my three-year-old boy. However, as I came to know more about Mr. Kuno, I came to like him less. He was a tyrant in the family. Perhaps it was a custom practised everywhere in that conservative region, but what surprised me greatly was their meal habit. Mr. Kuno ate alone in the living room at a small red lacquered table with his wife serving him, and when he was through, the rest of the family ate in the kitchen sitting on the wooden floor. Even their dishes were different.

Mrs. Kuno had deep lines between her eyebrows and she seemed to be restless all the time. One day, while I was in her living room having tea with her, she told me about her troubles with tears in her eyes.

Mr. Kuno had a mistress in Muramatsu and had two children by her. Mrs. Kuno could bear it if he kept secret about it, but he was proud of being able to keep a second wife, and what's more, he wanted his wife to become friends with his mistress and be nice to her children. One day the woman came to see him. "I couldn't stand it," Mrs. Kuno cried. I was very sorry for her.

"Besides," she continued, "my eldest daughter, Kazuko, was married and they were living with us. They had a boy. But my husband was not quite satisfied with her husband for some reason or other, and turned him out of the house and had them divorced. Poor Kazuko!"

Kazuko-san was about thirty and was a good-natured girl. Her son, the ten-year-old boy Ippei-chan was a nice boy, too. Mr. Kuno had turned the man out after they had an heir to the family. He loved Ippei-chan blindly and the grandchild was spoiled.

The second daughter, Sumiko-san also was a nice girl. She was serious and had good brains. The youngest daughter was attractive in the eyes of the American soldiers, but was a "flapper" according to the neighbors.

Mrs. Kuno was glad to have us staying with them, because, she said, "My husband stays at home more since you came. He doesn't spend so many nights at the woman's out of deference to you."

Later I learned more about Mr. Kuno from the mistress of a souvenir shop in the town who was Mr. Kuno's closest friend.

"I am very sorry for Mrs. Kuno," the lady said, "Her husband is a very jealous man. One day he came back from the woman's and found a guest bed ready in a room. Her relative had come to visit with her. When he saw it, he got very angry and unsheathing one of his swords, cut the bedding in two, and ran after his wife with the sword in his hand."

"He drinks *sake* at supper, and if something displeases him, he throws the table over and throws cups and plates at his wife."

I was horrified. Poor Japanese women! And yet, they dare not sue for divorce. Because, if they are divorced, the old Japanese civil law did not provide for their support from their former husband. Moreover, divorce is still considered a disgrace and the blame is almost always placed on the woman.

# Chapter 14

# MY DAYS AT THE STATION

I was enjoying myself very much. People of the station and the soldiers were very nice to me, and the people of the town, who I was afraid might turn their back on me, did not change their attitude toward me at all. On the contrary, they showed great interest in what I was doing, and came to ask me many questions. When I walked along the street, middle-school boys whispered to one another, "She is the interpreter", and small children greeted me with, "Hello!"

I did not lose their respect because I never went out with soldiers except on official business. We had many proposals for "dates" but I never accepted them, meeting with my American friends always at the station or at Mr. Kuno's where I lived.

Work at the station was enjoyable. Miss Kato—in love with Johnson—wanted to do the job all by herself so I remained mostly in the office as a receptionist. What I was to do was to sit in Mr. Kuno's office and enjoy talking with the visitors who were very frequent.

Of course, I was perfectly willing to do the baggage clerk's job, but when Johnson asked me to do something—which he often did—Miss Kato was not happy.

We had many visitors every day. The most frequent visitor was Lt. Grotious. Lt. Marlor, too, came very often. He was over thirty and was a composed, gentlemanly officer. He gave me a Japanese army raincoat and boots when he saw me standing in the rainy station yard without any covering. He acted like an elder brother to Lt. Grotious.

"He is just a kid," he would often say to me. But when they got together in teasing me, I had to run away. Although Lt. Marlor did not say much, he did not come to my rescue, just looking at my embarrassment with an amused look.

One day they came in and found me with Lt. Power. Although Mr. Kuno was with us, conversation was mostly between us two. Lt. Power was a heavy-set, bespectacled newspaperman whom I met a few days before on the train from Gosen.

It was in the evening. I was invited by Mr. Machida, the mayor and president, as Lt. Marlon and Lt. Grotious were coming. Lt. Power happened to be at the Gosen station, and the station master asked me to take him to Muramatsu.

Lt. Power asked me what I was. I told him I was an interpreter at the Muramatsu station, when he said, "Then, you are the pretty good girl at the station I have heard so much about." I said I was one of them.

Upon my telling him I was on my way to Mr. Machida's, he asked, "Is there going to be any entertainment?"

"No," I replied, "But Lt. Grotious alone can give us enough entertainment." Lt. Power was quite pleased with my answer.

"So, you have found your way here at last!" was Lt. Grotious's greeting to Lt. Power.

"Yes. Today I wanted to have female company, so I came to have a talk with Goto-san."

"Don't steal my girl away." Then Lt. Grotious became Lt. Ferocious.

"You are too popular. Garden is head over heels with you, and even Col. Payne was asking about you the other day at the party when you didn't come. Frost would do anything for you if you'd approach him with your womanly charm, and Higgins is another of your admirers. I have too many rivals."

Lt. Marlor as usual was smoking his pipe with an amused smile.

I rose to go.

"Where are you going?" Grotious-san said.

"I'm going to call for help."

"Whom are you going to call?"

"Miss Kato."

"She won't be of much help."

"But you can tease her while I can sit quietly."

Miss Kato did not like Lt. Grotious, who did not like her either, and he teased her about her love maliciously.

One day, we had a visit from two MPs. MPs here were not regular MPs but were picked out from among ordinary soldiers. They were two Mexican boys.

"Today it is our turn to stand guard at the station. So we came up to say hello to you," and the boys gave me some candies.

One of them I remembered well, but the other I could not identify, although he looked familiar to me.

"I think I have met you before, but I don't quite remember", I said.

"Yes. We came together the other day also," he said.

"He had his mustache shaved off by mistake at a barber's," explained his companion. We all laughed.

Soldiers were making friends with the people of the town. They preferred going to the town barber than to the barber at the camp. Families who had young girls often had visits from soldiers and they welcomed them. At the same time, we had come to notice quite a few "Off limits" signs in front of some houses—houses of ill fame—and painted women had increased in number.

It was not that I was talking nonsense all the time with the soldiers. Lt. Hoffman, the MP chief, was one of my more serious friends. He had been a teacher in New York. He was a good man, the three RTO boys said, but being the MP chief, he was considered too strict. He was interested in Japanese schools and came to ask us about education in Japan. One day we started an economic discussion.

"Japan is a small country and is overpopulated. We must send some of us to other lands," I said.

"No, it isn't necessary. You can live on without expanding. For..."

However, this was a subject that was out of scope and we had no data to back our argument. We exchanged a smile of relief when we were interrupted by another visitor.

Lt. Power as a newspaperman was naturally interested in what the people of the town thought of the American soldiers.

"What are they thinking about us? Do they resent us?" he asked.

"No. They were afraid of you in the beginning, it is true. But now they like you and are glad that it was you that came in. It is not only because you spend much money in the town buying souvenirs. They like American soldiers because they don't behave like victors. They like you because you are friendly, frank, and good-mannered. No complaint has been heard regarding your behavior. There was one case of a soldier stealing money from a girl with whom he spent the night, but as the soldier was duly punished, the people concerned were satisfied."

It was true. We heard of some soldiers who took some kimono from a farm house in the village, but nothing happened in the town and the soldiers as a whole were very well-behaved.

"People of the town were very much impressed with your jeeps and other machines like bulldozers. I heard them say 'No wonder we were beaten. America has such fine machines. It was very foolish of us to be thinking of fighting against Americans with bamboo spears as weapons.'"

"And those who have come to have close contact with you—for instance, people at the station—are surprised at and envious of the friendliness between officers and men. When an officer comes into a room where some soldiers are seated, they do not offer their seats promptly as Japanese soldiers were expected to do. They do not even stand up and salute. This is most amazing to the Japanese men who have spent some time in barracks, where beating was an everyday affair."

People were getting used to having American soldiers around. Many women had ceased to wear *mompe,* the wartime costume. In the beginning they carried their *mompe* in their bag and put it on when they came close to a place where soldiers were. One day when I was in the station yard giving directions to the engine driver in switching freight cars, an old woman in kimono came trotting down the street. She did not notice the soldiers until she came very near. Then she stopped, took out her *mompe* hurriedly and right in front of us put it on. It was at once laughable and pitiable.

Lt. Grotious did not have a high opinion of the Japanese in general. He laughed at the primitiveness of the way the farmers tilled the land, and he was amazed at the fact that although some cities were quite modern, people in the rural district led such primitive lives. It was harvest time in the district and rice plants were being cut and hung on the wooden bars.

"What are they doing?" he asked.

"They are being dried," I explained.

"How many days does it usually take for them to dry up?"

"A week or more."

"Why don't they make a common drying house without depending on the weather?"

I quite agreed with him.

# Chapter 15

# TO CHANGE IS THE ARMY WAY

One day, one of the baggage clerks came up with a pale face. He was trembling with excitement. He was a repatriated soldier and short-tempered. Fuming he said to me, "The baggage clerks at the Gosen station thundered at me because of the delay in giving them notice before shipping the freight cars out. 'What are you doing when you have two interpreters?' they said."

We explained to him that it was not our fault. We always let them know as soon as Johnson told us. But even Johnson-san did not know until the last moment, and besides, there were so many changes.

"Headache, headache, another headache!"

Very often he came up to us from his room downstairs, which used to be the baggage clerks' office.

"The car No. 1001 is not going to Niigata but to Takada."

"The box-car on the No. 1 track that I told you was ready to go out is not ready yet. Hold it till tomorrow."

"The car that is going out at 1:00 pm does not need a guard. Please have it locked and sealed."

Every time there was a change in order we had to rewrite the check sheet and inform the Gosen baggage clerks. It was not surprising that they got confused and became mad at us.

One day, Johnson told me to have seven carriages ready at Gosen by nine o'clock in the morning because some hundred new soldiers were coming. I relayed the order to Mr. Kuno. In order to have the seven carriages ready, they had to change the schedule of the trains for the whole line. It was a lot of trouble. But orders were orders. They arranged for it.

The next day I was at the Gosen station to meet the soldiers. They did come. But when they got off the train, a number of trucks appeared and carried them away to the barracks while the empty seven carriages stood waiting like fools.

I was vexed. I was sure I had not misunderstood Johnson. I said to him, "I suppose people at the station think that I made a mistake this time".

Johnson was vexed too. He said he was very sorry but neither did he expect to see the trucks.

"They phoned that no trucks were available today. To change is the Army way. We can't do anything about it ..."

## CHAPTER 16

# THE PARTY AT THE MAYOR'S

It was in the middle of October. The mayor, Mr. Machida, formally invited Col. Payne and his staff to his home.

Mr. Machida's house was a big house in the center of the town. Usually the main gate was closed and people went in and out of the small gate at the side of the house. But this evening the main gate was thrown open welcoming the honorable guests. Mr. and Mrs. Machida were in formal Japanese kimono, and Mrs. Machida who was a typical Japanese woman, reserved and shy, was very nervous. She said to me, "I don't want to sit at the table with the guests. Do you think it is all right if I retire soon after I am introduced?"

Mr. Tanaka, who was the chief interpreter at the camp and was there at the mayor's to help with the preparation, overheard this conversation and said, "Oh, no. You can't do that. You are the hostess and you must eat the food first to show that it is not poisoned. That is the custom, you know".

Mrs. Machida gave up the idea of retiring to her room, but begged me to stay by her and show her how to use knives and forks.

"You see I have never had a western-style dinner and I don't know how to eat properly."

She had been brought up in a wealthy family, and was a good-looking woman of about forty. She did not go out very much, and although people talked of her as being stuck-up, I felt that it was her shyness that kept her to her home and children. She had three children. A boy and two girls. The two girls, fifteen and ten, were in kimono tonight and were very charming.

"You must come out and bow to the guests," Mr. Machida, who once boasted about his popularity with geisha girls, was very fatherly tonight.

There were some eight or nine Japanese men, all in kimono and *hakama* (a kind of skirt men wear with their kimono on formal occasions). They were, beside Mr. Machida and Mr. Kuno, the chief of police and some important men of business. They all looked fine in kimono.

Girls who were to serve were picked out from our station office, the town office and the police station. They all were in beautiful kimono. Four of them were my friends at the office.

"I haven't worn kimono for a long time. Is my *obi* (sash) all right?"

"I don't know English at all. Please come to my rescue if I am spoken to."

They too were nervous and excited. They stood close together like so many little birds and wouldn't let me go. I said, "I shall have to serve them with *sake*, too. Show me how you do it, please".

They were experts at that and that made them feel more at ease.

"Put the plate first in front of the colonel and then serve the others."

They were rehearsing. Mr. Tanaka, the interpreter, was an excellent coach since he had once been a cook in New York.

Mr. Machida went out of the gate several times to see if the jeeps were coming. Mrs. Machida, her daughters, Mr. Kuno and two or three others and I lined up just inside the gate to welcome them.

"Here they are," Mr. Machida said.

One, two, three, four … four jeeps were coming with eight bright headlights brightening up the dark shops on each side one after another in succession.

There were about ten guests: Col. Payne, Col. Frost, Maj. Hazel Andrews and Maj. Turner, Capt. Mattison and Capt. Higgins, Lt. Loyte and Lt. Reed, with Sgt. Nishi as their interpreter.

Mr. Tanaka being busy in the kitchen, I introduced Mrs. Machida and her two daughters. The Americans thought the girls very charming and their kimono unusually beautiful. They asked how old they were and whether they liked school or not. The younger daughter, who was more courageous than her sister, declared she did not like mathematics. The older sister told them that she liked music, but when asked to sing a song, she hid her face with her long sleeves—a most womanly gesture that only Japanese women can do with their long sleeves—and ran away.

By this time, I had grown tired of the questions, "Where did you learn your English?" and "Have you ever been in the United States?" But again I had to tell the same thing.

"In 1937 I went over to the States to attend the Fourth America-Japan Student Conference that was held at Stanford University, California."

"No, we couldn't. We wanted very much to visit the East Coast also, but we had no time. We had to come back in time for the new semester."

"We landed at San Francisco. Then, after the conference was over, we visited Los Angeles, Portland, and Seattle."

"Oh, yes. Very much."

"How long did I stay? Exactly one month."

"Only one month! You speak excellent English," Col. Payne was amazed. Perhaps he did not realize that I had studied English at school and college.

Dinner was announced and we all moved into the dining room. There were no high tables and chairs but low Japanese tables and *zabuton* (cushions) to sit on.

Colonels sat in front of the alcove and next came the majors, captains, and then the lieutenants. Sgt. Nishi, by virtue of his being an interpreter, sat next to Maj. Andrews.

The party that at first was rather quiet because of the reserve on the part of the Japanese became hilarious as the number of bottles on the table increased. The chief of police was very popular with the Americans. The chief, with a red face and round startled-looking eyes was a heavy drinker.

"To the chief!" They raised their cups again and again. Each time the chief responded with a "Down the hatch!" and with "To Col. Payne", or "To Lt. Loyte".

***Taken at the Mayor's residence.***
***Japanese men are in formal kimono (except interpreters)***

*Mr. Machida is standing in the center with his two older girls while the youngest daughter is held by Col. Payne who sits next to Mrs. Machida. (The daughters are now back into their everyday costume.)*

*Seated in the front line between two Japanese girls in kimono is Col. Frost, with Mrs. Goto between the two colonels.*

*The young lady at the extreme left is a geisha girl. So are the three girls (one standing) toward the right. The other three girls are from station office. Mr. Kuno is standing (4th from the left).*

*The round wooden object in front is a Japanese charcoal stove.*

Lt. Hoyte, who was a young officer, did not drink at all, but he seemed to enjoy the party just as much as the others.

There was another officer who did not drink. It was Maj. Hazel who sat quietly between the heavy drinkers, Maj. Turner and Capt. Higgins. He said he was a Catholic and that is why he did not drink. Lt. Hoyte also was a Catholic.

I was impressed with the strong influence it has on the daily life of its followers. Their life is regulated by religion. God is omnipotent in America while Japanese gods stay only in shrines and at altars. Very few Japanese people are really religious. Those who visit shrines and temples are many, but they go to ask Gods or Buddhas for their favors for themselves and members of their families—selfish motives—and religion is only formality with them and they don't practice its teachings conscientiously in their daily life.

Americans generally seem to think that Shintoism is our national religion and that most Japanese are Shintoists. But it is not true. There are two kinds of Shintoism. One is an established religion followed by a minority while the other—which is understood by most Americans as Shintoism—is merely ancestor worship. Imperial ancestors and some of our forefathers who did meritorious deeds for the country are enshrined, and we visit the shrines to pay our homage. They are not real gods in the true sense. However, as it is in human nature to attribute divinity to something beyond our comprehension, we have come to think of the departed souls as having supernatural influence and have come to pray for the favor and protection of our "gods."

During the war, the government authorities said that the "Divine Wind" would blow and lead us to victory, and the shrines were thronged with visitors. But now that we suffered a defeat, some of the shrines are reported to be left deserted. This shows that people are disappointed in our gods. If they truly believed in "Shintoism," now should be the time for them to visit shrines and pray for guidance, I think.

What a shrine means to most Japanese is a place where they are wed, while a Buddhist temple is always connected with funerals and graves. There are not many public cemeteries in Japan. Consequently, a Japanese Christian may be wed at a shrine and buried in a graveyard belonging to a temple.

Just as I was philosophizing to myself, I heard Major Turner say, "I am high." So was everyone else who drank. Girls were busy going back and forth between the kitchen and the dining room. They laughed when the police chief said something in his one-month-old English, and were obviously enjoying the party, too.

Mr. Machida stood up with a piece of paper in his hand and read a welcome speech, and Col. Payne expressed thanks on behalf of those who were invited.

After that entertainments began. A group of small girls around the age of twelve or so, all dressed up in beautiful kimono, danced Japanese dances to delight the eyes of the foreign guests. They were very cute and were met with a great applause. When they withdrew, four women appeared and danced to the accompaniment of a *samisen* (three-stringed musical instrument).

"They were formerly geisha girls," one of the girls whispered to me, "During the war they were working in Mr. Mori's factory." Mr. Mori, who was present, had brought them here to entertain.

When their program was over, they were invited to sit with the guests. There was much noise and laughter when they chose their seats. Majors, captains, and lieutenants, all wanted to call them to their side. Three of them were pretty young girls while the one who was the best dancer was not so young and not good-looking at all. When I expressed my surprise, my friends said, "But she is the No. 1 of the town." Good looks alone does not make a good geisha girl, I realized.

After this, the party became more and more boisterous and I became very busy. They were asking many questions of the girls, and they all needed an interpreter.

Once I was engaged in a talk with Maj. Hazel who did not drink occasionally pouring *sake* into Capt. Higgins' cup. I was just reaching for a bottle when somebody called me. Answering I took up the bottle and poured it. Capt. Higgins drank it and his boyish face made such an indescribable expression. I couldn't help bursting out laughing—I realized the bottle contained Japanese tea for Maj. Hazel.

Suddenly, Col. Frost who had been looking pale for some time vomited. Drinking Japanese *sake* and beer at the same time was bad for him.

At this Col. Frost got mad. He grew so angry that he threw away the cake on his plate in a sulky childish way, saying it was a disgrace for an American officer to throw up in front of the Japanese people.

A sudden awkward silence filled the room. It was very embarrassing. We all tried to appease Col. Payne after Col. Frost was helped out of the room.

"It is not considered a disgrace in Japan, because one just can't help it."

"We are to blame for serving him *sake* to which he is not accustomed."

We tried very hard, but his rage was not quenched, when the oldest geisha came forward and took care of him talking to him in Japanese. Col. Payne who was now on his feet held her by the arm and said, "If this girl is trying to entice me, I am going with her."

I was annoyed. Mr. Tanaka was not there, and no other Japanese there could understand what he said. Wishing that I hadn't been able to understand English I fled to the kitchen to call Mr. Tanaka who was enjoying his *sake* all by himself.

I remained there for a few minutes telling the girls not to go in for a while. When I came back to the room Col. Payne was not there. He was taken upstairs to have a rest, I was told. I felt relieved to find the girl still in company. Someone was saying that a *Jinrikisha* (rickshaw) was sent for another girl.

People who became sober for a while began to drink afresh to forget about it.

"Harumi! Harumi!" Capt. Higgins, a big twenty-four-year old man who pouted when he spoke, was calling to one of the geisha girls who was most coquettish. She was very popular and when she sat with Capt. Higgins, someone on the opposite side of the U-shaped table jealously called her back. Finally she sat in the middle and would not go to either of them.

"Tell your *teishu* (husband) ... Your *kamisan* (wife) is ..."

Sgt. Nishi was talking to Mr. and Mrs. Machida. It was amusing. For, the words *teishu* and *kamisan* are usually used by people of lower social standing. Japan is considered to be still in the stage of feudalism compared with western countries, and the relics of feudalism are best noticed in the language. In the olden times, there were four established classes—warriors, farmers, artisans, and merchants. Their intermarriage was forbidden, and the language they spoke differed. Especially the personal pronouns varied according to people's social standing. Even today, husbands of upper classes are called *danna-sama* or *go-shujin-sama* meaning master and their wives *okusama,* while *teishu* and *kamisan* are used referring to husbands and wives of merchants, artisans, and farmers.

Mrs. Machida, with her quiet dignity, certainly was not a *kamisan*. I felt sorry for Sgt. Nishi because it revealed without his telling it that his Japanese-speaking parents were not of higher social standing. Nisei people sometime make such blunders.

The fat, middle-aged Major Turner was walking around in Mr. Kuno's *haori* (coat). Not being very tall, he looked quite becoming in it.

Dancing was suggested, and some stood up and danced with the geisha girls. Even the chief of police was dancing in a clumsy way. I wondered where he could have learned it. Singing also began. Every one joined in "Old Kentucky Home" and the girls were eager to learn new songs like "You Are My Sunshine."

After Col. Payne was gone, it was no longer a formal party. They left their seats and made groups of twos and threes, drinking, talking, and singing.

The clock in the kitchen struck eleven. Mr. Tanaka told us girls to go home. I went back to the dining room to see if Mr. Kuno was ready to go home. There was no train anymore and Mr. Kuno and I were to go home together by car. Fortunately he was willing to leave. During the evening, he had kept mostly to his Japanese friends, and, as he had had enough drinking, he was satisfied.

The car being ready I left them "high" up in heaven wondering when they would come down to the earth.

# Chapter 17

# OHARA-SAN AND MAKINO-SAN

It was one of those days when our business slackened—no freight cars came in, and there was nothing to ship out. I went home for lunch as usual. It took me only seven minutes to get to Mr. Kuno's where I lived, and I usually took the 12:55 pm train to come back to Muramatsu. But sometimes I missed it. One day, I saw it come in. It stays at Gosen for five minutes. So I thought I didn't have to make haste.

But I was alarmed to hear the whistle when I was putting on my shoes. I dashed to the station to see the train already some hundred meters off. I had to get back to Muramatsu in time. Some sick soldiers were leaving for a Sendai hospital and Miss Kato did not show up that morning. In a flurry, I told it to the station master, who had his men yell, and the train came back. I felt like some important person.

Today, however, I made it with ease and came back to the office to find Miss Kato, Johnson, and Grey waiting for me. They were going to see a show at the only theater in the town. Noriko Awaya and her band had come down from Tokyo. But I wasn't much interested in jazz, so I declined the invitation.

It was not dull at all staying in the office. They were not always busy and the girls were learning English with the army conversation book that someone had given them. I enjoyed talking with the girls. In the beginning I was surprised to hear them use the same pronouns men did. But I understood it was their dialect, and I was getting used to it.

They were young girls about twenty years of age. Miss Shirai, Mr. Kuno's secretary, and Miss Murata were the oldest—twenty-two—and they were pretty. I was shocked to hear the rumor that Miss Shirai was another mistress of Mr. Kuno's. "Impossible," I said to my husband, who reminded me that Niigata Prefecture is famous for its production of "snow-white beauties"—geisha girls—and becoming a geisha and living a luxurious life is not considered a disgrace. "I cannot believe it," I said to one of the girls, who said, "I don't know. But he takes her along with him when he goes on a trip sometimes."

At any rate, she and Miss Murata were beautiful girls, and I was rather surprised to know that Miss Nakamura and Miss Kaneko who were not considered beauties among Japanese were more popular with the soldiers. Miss Nakamura was a slim, dark-complexioned girl and looked like a Filipina except for her slant eyes. Miss Kaneko was cute. She was only fifteen or so and was always ready to smile or to laugh. She was the one who served tea to visitors. Lt. Grotious had much fun teasing her.

"Shorty! Kaneko-san! Come here. You are my *koibito* (sweetheart)." So saying, he chased her round the desks while she ran away laughing.

As I was looking out of the window at the snow-clad mountains far away, Mr. Kuno, who had gone downstairs to see what Howard was doing alone, came up and asked me to come down with him to the room where the RTO boys stayed. There were three boys whom I had never met before. Howard introduced them as his friends. They were young boys—just as young as Howard—and they wanted to buy some ivory carvings and wished to know where they could get them.

When I told this to Mr. Kuno, he promptly offered to take them to the shop he knew. It was in the town of Gosen. From the station we took a short cut by way of going through Mr. Kuno's yard, and we had hardly walked a minute or two when Kazuko-san, the eldest girl, came running after us. We turned back to see some soldiers in front of the Kuno house. Kazuko-san said that they were saying "knife" and *katana* (sword). "I was scared," she said.

We went back to find out what was up. The soldiers said they were going back home in a few days and that they wanted to buy swords as souvenirs. They saw us coming out of the gate and went in to see if it was a shop.

"Shall we go together?" I suggested. The three boys said "OK" rather reluctantly.

Now we were a group of about fifteen. And when we walked together a crowd of children followed us keeping a reserved distance. When we came to the main street, the soldiers went into the first shop thanking us for showing the way.

Mr. Kuno took the three boys to the shop of which he apparently was one of the best customers. Seeing Mr. Kuno, the master of the shop took out many beautiful lacquer wares and ivory carvings. The boys were just excited. "Wonderful! Wonderful!" "Look at this incense box!" "Isn't it precious!"

They wanted to buy everything.

"Which do you like best?"

"I'll take this if it's all right with you."

"I'll take this one. Mother will like it very much."

They picked up some ten pieces worth thousands of yen, then hesitated a little and turned to me saying,

"Mrs. Goto. We have not enough money now. We were told that we'd get paid in a few days. Will he keep these things for us until we come back in two or three days?"

The shopkeeper was willing to do so. They were very happy and thanked Mr. Kuno for the privilege they could enjoy.

This was my first encounter with Ohara-san and Makino-san who became our family friends. The three boys were Messrs. Carr, O'Hara, and MacKinnon, and as O'Hara and MacKinnon sounded like the Japanese names "Ohara" and "Makino" we came to call them "Ohara-san" and "Makino-san".

***Ohara-san, Private First Class from Milwaukee, Makino-san, Private First Class from Milwaukee***

They were college students. Ohara-san was interested in philosophy and Makino-san was a medical student. They were unanimous in loathing the war and the army. They were within a few days' reach of Okinawa when they heard the news of Japan's surrender on board. They were very happy because they did not have to participate in fighting. The two were very good friends although their interests were not always the same.

Ohara-san was of a more serious type while Makino-san was just what we expected a young American college student to be—full of life and enjoying it as best he could. What brought them so closely together was the fact that they were both from the same town—Milwaukee.

After that, they came to see us very often.

When *konban-wa* (Good evening) with an emphasis on *ban* was heard in the direction of the entrance hall, it was always my boy, Ken-chan, who ran downstairs ahead of us to meet them. They were shown into the Kuno's living room where we joined them and had a pleasant hour or two together.

Sometimes they came every night. I was surprised and asked.

"I heard that you are allowed to come out only three times a week. How do you manage to get out?"

They exchanged a smiling look.

"We don't pay any attention to orders. We come out through a hole in the hedge."

"The other night we were just about to squeeze through, when—who do you think came? It was Col. Payne. We jumped into the bush to hide."

They seemed to be the most frequent visitors at the curio shops in Gosen. Shopkeepers all knew "Ohara-san" and "Makino-san". Sometimes the boys ran out of money, and then it was cigarettes, soap, candies and rations that they traded with. One day, they brought Japanese army leather gloves and slippers to trade. I asked with rounded eyes, "How did you get them?"

"In the warehouse, there are hundreds and hundreds of them. Officers always take them out. Why not we?" was Makino-san's reply. He used to say, "Mrs. Goto, tell me anything you need. Can you get sugar and butter? If you need them I'll bring them next time." And they did. It was through their kindness that Ken-chan and Ippei-chan, the Kuno boy, could enjoy more sweets than any other children in the town. They spoiled Ken-chan. While talking, they would let him sit on their laps, and Ken-chan still calls a kiss on the forehead "Doing Makino-san".

Unlike many other Catholic soldiers who refrained from drinking, Ohara-san had no compunction in drinking *sake*. He liked it very much and so did Makino-san. They complained that while officers had plenty to drink, ordinary soldiers had none, and they enjoyed Mr. Kuno's *sake* with relish.

Ohara-san was brought up in a very good family. Makino-san said, "Ohara's family is one of the wealthiest in Milwaukee, and his girlfriend is of a family who is just as rich as the Mitsui, the wealthiest family in Japan."

Makino-san said Ohara-san was a very fine pianist. He had

slender fingers like those of a woman, and we could easily believe it. But then, Ohara-san told us that Makino-san was a great singer. We all asked him to sing for us.

"Ohara-san. *Uta, dozo*," (please sing) Kazuko-san said.

"*Dozo, dozo*!" Mrs. Kuno joined.

Ohara-san was convulsed with laughter, while Makino-san protested. The fact was he couldn't sing.

"I can't sing. Out of tune" , he said, laughing bashfully like a nice-looking girl.

Mrs. Kuno always served her guests with various kinds of Japanese food. Dried persimmon was everybody's favorite, while dried squid was most Americans' abhorrence. Makino-san, however, liked it.

"It is good," he said to Ohara-san. "Why don't you try it?" But Ohara-san declined politely.

One evening Ohara-san came alone. When the Kuno family told him to come in as usual, he said to me, "Tonight I came to ask a few questions of Mr. Goto. I want to know something about Oriental philosophy."

My husband happened to be a student of Chinese political philosophy, so I showed him into our room upstairs. My husband, who made frequent trips to Tokyo to take his papers to a research institute where he worked, seldom joined the company downstairs even when he was with us. Although he enjoyed my chatting about soldiers, he always preferred to stay upstairs when I joined the company in Mr. Kuno's living room. But that night when I announced Ohara-san's visit, he was good enough to spare a couple of hours for the aspiring student.

Finding Ken-chan a great nuisance, we spent the evening in a quiet talk. Makino-san went to see a movie show but Ohara-san was not interested in the movies. He wanted to find out what we thought of the Emperor.

"Is it true that you look up to him as a living god?"

"Some Japanese do. But not we. We knew he is just an ordinary human being with virtues and faults just like ourselves. We feel sorry for him. But we wish he had had a little more willpower and had not allowed the militarists to start the war."

However, I could not help feeling shocked to hear Ohara-san call him "Hirohito". For a moment I could not realize who it was. He had always been "His Imperial Majesty" to us.

"How did you feel when the war ended?"

"Naturally we felt very happy when we realized what it meant," I said.

On that memorable fifteenth of August, 1945, we all gathered around the radio and listened in, for it had been announced the day before that a very important broadcast would be made. When the broadcast began, we did not realize at first that it was the Emperor himself speaking to us. When I realized it, and knew what he was telling us, something hot and then cold ran through my body and I could not stay with the others. I ran upstairs and cried very hard. When the broadcast was over my husband came up and said in a composed voice, "Don't cry, silly girl! Didn't you know that this would be a natural consequence?"

I had anticipated it. My father, my husband and brothers—all were pessimistic even from the very beginning of the war. They were sure Japan would lose. I had enough sense to know they were right. But I was a patriot. I loved my country. Every time the national bonds were issued I bought some, disregarding my husband's advice.

However, I knew the announcements of the Imperial Headquarters were false when I listened to the radio the day after our house was burnt. A B-29 flew over and dropped some incendiary bombs destroying 500 houses and killing three people. But the radio said, "No damage"!

It was with mixed feelings that we listened in to the Emperor's broadcast. But the feeling of relief was far greater than any other emotion. We could now enjoy the beauty of the sky day and night without any fear. No threatening sound of an alarm siren would disturb our sleep.

During the few weeks after the surrender, many rumors were spread. A policeman's wife in the neighborhood was knowingly telling us that the Army and Navy's joint airforce was planning a last counterattack on the American forces when they approached the main land and that a part of the Army was rioting in Tokyo. But we were not interested; "No more, no more of war," was our honest voice.

Ohara-san was seriously interested in Japan and the Japanese, and he had started to learn the language. He always had a pencil and paper in his pocket, and whenever he heard a word he was likely to use often, he would write it down in his notebook. Makino-san, too, was trying to learn it, but his happy-go-lucky nature didn't let him take it so seriously as did Ohara-san.

Makino-san with his good looks and open-heartedness, and Ohara-san with his red face, eye-glasses, and his peculiar way of opening his mouth before he spoke, along with his well-bred seriousness, were gradually winning our hearts. We came to consider them as real friends and not mere "soldier-friends." Ohara-san, who came to see us every Sunday after all of us went back to Tokyo, is still our very good friend whose development we like to watch from across the Pacific.

## Chapter 18

# DISMAYED

One day I was asked by one of the drivers to take his clothes to the laundry. He had no time. The shop was on my way home, and the laundryman and I were good chatting friends ever since I had pointed out some mistakes in his hurriedly put-up English signboard in front of the shop. "Creaning" for "Cleaning" was one of the mistakes, and there were all kinds of funny mistakes in English. I told him, after pointing them out, not to change it because I noticed that soldiers enjoyed the impossible English. As I thought, this shop flourished much more than the other two laundry shops in the town.

So it was to this shop that I took the driver's clothes.

"Two shirts, two trousers, three handkerchiefs."

He took a memo down while his four small daughters were happily eating candies I brought for them. Because of my bribery the laundryman always had my clothes ready on time when I called for them. Then, he turned all the pockets over to see if there was anything left in them. Together with some crumpled pieces of paper, he fished out something yellow.

"I wonder what this is," he said and pushed it toward me. It was made of rubber, and with dismay, I realized what it was.

"Oh, it's for his finger. Bandage, you know. He cut his finger by mistake," I said hurriedly. "Give it to me with those pieces of paper. I'll give them back."

The laundryman wrapped it up with paper and handed it to me.

"Then, by tomorrow evening, please."

"Yes, Ma'am. Thank you very much for the candies."

I did not turn back to say *sayonara*. "How shall I dispose of it?" occupied my mind. I couldn't return it to Johnson. I wished the laundryman had known and had not asked me such an embarrassing question like he did. At the same time, however, I reflected that the ignorance of this sort might be a reason for our overpopulation. Thinking, I turned a corner and there I was on a bridge. Without a moment's hesitation, I threw it, with paper and all, in the water. It went floating down the river giving me a great relief. I hope none of those pieces of paper was of any importance to the driver.

# Chapter 19

## THE NEW RTO BOYS

"Goodbye, Mrs. Goto!"

"*Sayonara,* Miss Kato!"

Grey-san and Howard-san came up to shake hands with us.

"Why? Where are you going?" we asked, quite surprised.

"We are going back to the camp."

"Was anything wrong?"

"No. You know this is an officer's job and too important a job for ordinary privates. But our commander likes us and has been letting us take charge of it. But if we stay any longer we will be assigned to some other unit. And he doesn't want to lose us, so he is calling us back. But we can come out anytime we want, because we have a pass. Besides, Johnson is going to stay."

They really seemed very sorry to leave us. The station people were also sorry to see them go back to the camp. The two had made good friends with the people at the station. Station master, baggage clerks, ticket girls, all liked them well and had given them nicknames "O-chame-san" (Playful One) and "Odebu-chan" (Fatty) respectively to Grey and Howard.

"So long! See you again!"

They caught a passing jeep and went away throwing kisses to us. We all stood at the window and saw them off until Howard's smiling broad face and Grey's newly bought red silk handkerchief turned the corner at the police station and disappeared out of sight.

New boys were already at the station when we came to work on the following morning. Both of them were dark-colored, black-haired boys. Mr. Limon was Spanish type, very thin and gave me a rather sickly impression with his two large black eyes glittering passionately. Mr. Roderiguez was younger and he was very dark like a Mexican native. He had, however, fine features and was always smiling good-naturedly.

In the afternoon Miss Kato was taking a pattern of the soldier's cap. Her friend thought it was very nice and wanted to know how it was made. When Mr. Limon came up and saw it, he said he would give her one of his caps since he had two. I was much surprised. Giving his cap away to a foreign girl! If a Japanese soldier did such a thing, he would get court-martialed.

Mr. Kuno proposed to have a welcome party for the newcomers. So, in the evening, we all went to Gosen to a Japanese restaurant in a quiet corner of the town that we learned with interest was the gay quarters. I had never been in such a place. I looked around to see if I could get a glimpse of a geisha girl in her formal business costume, but the houses behind the black wooden walls on both sides were as quiet as ordinary houses and no merry sound reached my disappointed ears. We went into a gate, and beyond a few stepping stones and shrubbery, we found the house flooded with light.

"*Irasshaimashi*!" Two or three women ran out to meet us. Mr. Kuno had already informed them of our coming.

Mr. Johnson who had been at a Japanese home several times stooped down and was pulling at his shoe strings. Limon-san followed, but brown Roderiguez-san just stood at the threshold and would not come in.

"Why don't you come in?"

He said something in Spanish. Limon-san told us that he didn't want to take off his shoes. If he must take off his shoes he was going back to the station. I could not help smiling. It sounded so childish.

But at the same time I felt sorry noticing his obvious embarrassment.

When the women of the restaurant were told what the trouble was, they said, "Please come up with your shoes on."

Roderiguez was very happy, and even Johnson and Limon, who were already out of their shoes, put them on again.

It was very nice of the restaurant people to let them come up with their shoes on, I thought, looking at the heavy boots trodding on the corridor floor polished like a mirror.

When I think of it now, I realize that our psychology works the other way round. After the American dependents came to Tokyo, many western-style houses owned by wealthy Japanese were taken as homes for American personnel. When we are invited to come to their home, we can't help experiencing a little hesitation at the door before we go in with our shoes on. We look down at our shoes in spite of ourselves, which are not so clean as a car-riding American's shoes, and we feel kind of sheepish.

One day, Ken-chan and I were invited to visit an American couple and their two-year-old son. They lived in a hotel. When the door was opened and we were asked to come in, Ken-chan took his tiny shoes off and put them tidily in the corridor before going into the room.

Now, Mr. Kuno and we were shown into a quiet twelve-mat room upstairs. It was the first time for the new boys, being in a Japanese house. They felt the *tatami* (smooth straw mats two or three inches thick that cover the floor) and looked around the room curiously.

We sat at a long low table. The boys sat in front of the alcove with Johnson in the middle, and Mr. Kuno, Kazuko, the eldest Kuno girl, Miss Kato and I sat on the other sides. Beer and *sake* were brought in with various kinds of Japanese food. With an air of expertise, Johnson showed them how to handle chopsticks. Limon could do all right, but poor Roderiguez was very clumsy and could not hold them properly. In the end, he gave up his efforts and took up the fork that we had ordered as a precaution. He was bashful over the reluctance he showed at taking his shoes off and his clumsiness in managing to eat with chopsticks. We could not help liking him better for that.

***Roderiguez-san who did not want to take off his shoes.***

Limon was also rather a quiet boy. But his sparkling black eyes expressed eloquently the fact that he was enjoying himself. Kazuko-san was sitting in front of him, and although she knew only a few words of English, each was apparently enjoying the other's company—this I realized some time afterward.

The dinner was good and abundant. When we came out, the moon was up and it was a beautiful evening.

"It really is a *buenos noches,* isn't it?" I said to Limon-san.

Roderiguez walking alone a few steps behind us was whistling a Spanish tune. We walked slowly inhaling the lovely evening air.

After a few minutes, we came out of the dark alley to the lighted street. There was a small theater.

"Let's go in", quick-tempered Mr. Kuno said. Before we could say "Yes" or "No", he was already buying tickets.

Miss Kato and I were alarmed.

"But, Mr. Kuno, it's off limits!" we cried.

"Never mind. I am taking them in." He was a little tipsy.

The boys looked to see if an MP was around. Then, in a moment, their alert figures were behind the door.

It was a full house. We went upstairs to have a better view of the stage where a small girl in red kimono was dancing a Japanese dance.

"Phew ...", Johnson whistled with delight. Limon and Roderiguez also looked very happy.

When the dance was over, a girl in a blue evening dress came out and stood behind the microphone. The boys clapped their hands enthusiastically.

After that, a band of white uniformed musicians appeared and played jazz music. The boys' excitement reached its climax. By this time, they had all stood up and now Johnson started to dance in a little space behind us. Limon and Roderiguez, too, joined the band with singing when they played "La Paloma," which was very popular in Japan.

It was really an unexpected treat for them.

## Chapter 20

# A LITTLE TACT TO STOP GOSSIP

One afternoon, I was out in the road in front of the station with Mr. Kuno. There was a warehouse nearby, and a woman, pulling a hand wagon toward it, was hit by an army truck. She was not hurt at all but the wagon was split in two. We were negotiating with the soldiers of the truck to get some compensation for the woman.

She was the owner of a tiny confectionery in the town. She had a married daughter in a city who had asked her mother to be the custodian of her kimono during the war, because she did not need them and she was afraid her house might be burned. Fortunately her house did not receive any damage during the air-raids and now she asked her mother to send her kimono back. So, the kind mother had packed the kimono in wooden boxes, borrowed a wagon from her neighbor and dragged the heavy wagon to the station. It was estimated by an onlooker that it would cost fifty yen to have the wagon repaired.

"I can't return the broken wagon to my neighbor. But I can't afford to pay fifty yen for the repair. What shall I do?"

She cast a worried look at the broken wagon, at the truck driver, and then at us.

The driver was sorry. He said he would file a report to his superior officer and would try to have the woman compensated. "But it will take some time," he added. Nothing further could be done at the moment, so we had only to withdraw.

Later I realized it was careless of me not to have asked the driver's name. The woman came up two or three times to ask what had become of it. Each time I cycled to the liaison office at the police station to inquire only to be disappointed. "No, we haven't received any notice from the camp yet," was the answer. In the end, I apologized to the woman for my carelessness and gave her some money, which she accepted with a repeated, "I'm sorry."

It rained hard the day before and the road was very muddy. When we were about to come back to the station office I heard a jeep coming and in order to avoid being splashed I stepped aside to one side of the road. However, the jeep suddenly pulled up and I was seized by the arm by somebody in the jeep.

"Hello, Sweetness!" It was Lt. Grotious. "I'm going to Gosen. Won't you come with me?"

I turned to Mr. Kuno to see what he would say. He could deny nothing to his favorite "Lt. Budoshu-san."

"I am looking for some silk. Do you know a good place?"

Mr. Kuno knew everything about the town of Gosen. He told us to go to a certain small factory where they were weaving silk. They did not sell to casual visitors, but his name card would serve as a pass.

The road from Muramatsu to Gosen was a good road, and it was very pleasant driving through the paddies.

The autumnal sky seemed higher and bluer after the rain. In the distance were the peaks of mountains changing their color from bluish green to purple when a passing cloud cast its shadow on them. The highest peak was already snow-clad.

The rice hung in rows on high bars like golden screens hiding green groves and brown thatched roofs of farm houses as we passed by.

We found the factory without any difficulty. We went to the owner's house next door. The door was opened by a middle-school boy who beamed to find an American soldier standing at his door. It was a good opportunity for him to speak English.

"Good afternoon," he began. "What...", then he was stuck. I knew he wanted to say "What can I do for you?" But, poor boy, as the English language was almost struck out of the school curriculum during the war, "Good afternoon" was all he could fish out of his limited vocabulary. He turned imploringly to me.

When I told him about the lieutenant's objective in coming here, the boy called his mother. "Mother! Mother! Here's an American officer who wants to buy silk."

His mother was a nice elderly lady. When I told her that Mr. Kuno had sent us here, she went in to the interior of the house, telling the boy to give us cushions to sit on.

The mother came back with a tea tray and some rolls of silk. Lt. Grotious picked out a beautiful cream colored silk for his mother.

"Not for your girlfriend?"

"No."

"*Ikura desu ka*?" he asked in Japanese. When the mother told him it was 300 yen, he turned to me with, "Do you have some money with you? I haven't brought enough money."

"No, I don't. I don't carry so much money with me all the time. (Things were still cheap then.) Shall we go to Mr. Kuno's and borrow some money from Mrs. Kuno?"

Lt. Grotious patronizingly patted me on the shoulder, laughing.

"Don't take everything so seriously. I was just kidding. But that's why I like you."

"*Domo arigato, mata dozo*" (Thank you very much. Please again), said Lt. Grotious in his funny way, and we left the house hearing the delighted laughter of the mother and boy, who, I felt sure, would boast about his experience to all his classmates the next day.

We walked through the narrow alley. When we walked side by side Lt. Grotious was a foot taller than I was.

"You are a small girl," he said, looking down .

"You are a long boy," I retorted, looking up.

After a few steps of silence, he suddenly said, "They are talking about us."

"Who?"

"Officers, naturally."

"Then, I don't care...."

"But you are not the object of scandal yet."

"Yet? Do you mean to say that I am going to be?"

Lt. Grotious smiled a reluctant smile.

There were only three English-speaking girls in the district. Miss Kato, myself, and a Nisei girl at a police station some ten miles away from Muramatsu. Lt. Grotious had met her several times, and once he said to me pityingly, "She is crazy."

"Why? Captain Dodds?" I asked, having heard that she came to visit the captain at the camp. Lt. Grotious nodded.

Although he kidded me once saying, "Let's go somewhere and stay overnight," he did not like the kind of girl who would actually do so. When he said it, I was so taken aback that I just stared at him saying nothing. Johnson-san, who was with us, burst out laughing and said for me, "Never happen!"

Miss Kato's love for Johnson was quite well known. I was to blame for it, because my tongue slipped in front of Ferocious Grotious who spread the news among his ill-tongued friends.

She kept Johnson's picture in her purse, and on her desk was a picture of herself with Johnson and Grey. When Johnson was out in the yard she was out in the yard also. And when she was not to be found in the office, people said, "Go and look in Johnson-san's room."

She took a day off once and went to the city of Niigata to have a permanent wave done. And she elaborately painted her cheeks and lips, which was the object of Ferocious Grotious's teasing.

I was a little concerned for Miss Kato. She seemed to be desperate sometimes and she drank a great deal, often going out to restaurants with soldiers. Mr. Kuno being an amorous man himself, was interested in her love for Johnson and was trying to put them together. I knew Johnson did not take it seriously and he was a quite respectable man; but if she was going to stay here long, it wouldn't be good for her to be gossiped about.

It was true that Lt. Grotious and I were good friends and enjoyed joking with each other. But I didn't want to be the object of gossip. So I looked for a chance to put an end to it.

One day, I found Lt. Butler in Johnson's room. He was another good friend of Lt. Grotious and was the commander of the 1st company. He was a thin, jocular man, and his face looked like Popeye the Sailor Man. He was popular among the soldiers also. The first time I met him, I did something that made him come up to joke with me whenever he came to the station.

I went up to Lt. Grotious, who was chatting with a lieutenant, whom he introduced as Lt. Butler.

"Do you know that Mr. Johnson has a girl in his room?" I said, They exchanged a wondering glance. Lt. Butler, who was Johnson's chief, was naturally concerned. They went toward his room hurriedly and dubiously. Miss Kato and I followed, chuckling. It was a scroll of a life-size picture of a standing girl in kimono—Mr. Kuno's present.

"You liar!" they shouted at me.

As soon as I finished talking with Johnson about the car, Lt. Butler began, "They say you like Grotious."

"I do," I admitted.

"But I like Lt. Marlor, Lt. Butler, Lt. Power, Lt. Garden and many others too."

"Do you know whom you are talking with?" Johnson asked.

"Yes. Lt. Butler. I can't help liking all those who are nice to me. And as everybody is nice to me, I can't help liking everybody," I said.

"You speak like a geisha girl," Lt. Butler said, smiling in spite of himself. But I saw he was not displeased.

I did not ask Lt. Grotious whether they stopped talking about us. But after that, Mr. Kuno's home received a number of new visitors. So I knew my tact was successful.

# CHAPTER 21

# SOUVENIR SHOPS

They were indeed the men of the renowned Regiment. The soldiers as a whole behaved themselves admirably. People of the town began to like them more and more as they came to know them better.

In the beginning they were frightened, not knowing what kind of people Americans were. By and by, however, they came to find out that the American soldiers were very nice people—cheerful, friendly, magnanimous, and kind to small children. They were childlike themselves. They ate and whistled in the street—especially at pretty girls—and loved to sit on railings. I often saw them sitting on the railings of the bridge in front of the station or on the wicket at the entrance to the platform while waiting for the train. They looked like birds perched on a boar. Such kinds of behavior were considered ill-mannered among Japanese, but with those carefree soldiers, it looked very natural.

What struck the Japanese as a characteristic of Americans was that all of them without exception carried a picture of his wife or sweetheart. After a few minutes of acquaintance they would take out their pictures and cherishingly showed them around. In the train, at a souvenir shop, or in a private home, Japanese people were shown pictures of many American women.

"They must be longing for home very badly," townspeople said remembering our unrepatriated soldiers abroad.

On the other hand, Americans were surprised to find no trace of resentment or malice on the part of the natives.

"We were prepared to meet some violence or at least resistance and we were quite surprised because Japanese people are so peaceful and hospitable to us," one of them remarked.

The Japanese are a peace-loving people, but their attachment to the Emperor was so strong that they did anything they were ordered to do in his name. They fought desperately because they were told that it was for his sake; they threw away their arms when the Emperor told them to do so. They had not felt particular enmity against Americans; it was through elaborate propaganda that they came to hate America.

The Japanese are an emotional people. They do not do much reasoning. Everything for the Emperor! This attitude is seen in a smaller scale in their daily life. They pay particular attention to their own family or personal friends and give less consideration to strangers. When getting on a train they would push others away and occupy seats for their companions. They don't care if a woman with heavy baggage is standing in front of them. Indeed, loyalty and filial piety have been our two outstanding virtues. Just as our language is written lengthways, so did we pay attention only to the vertical order of society without looking sideways at our fellow human beings.

As it was with a sense of relief that we were shaken out of our long nightmarish dream, it was not surprising that people generally showed no enmity or resentment against the Americans when they knew that they did no harm to innocent people. At the same time, they realized that it was the best opportunity for them to make money.

Souvenir shops appeared like bamboo shoots after a rain. A widow I knew kept a small fancy goods store and was very pessimistic when the coming of the troops was announced. She thought of retiring in their native village. However, when I dropped in to see her after a month or so, she told me excitedly about the money she made during one month.

***A part of the shopping district of Muramatsu as it used to be.***

A "Souvenir Shop" sign was pasted on the window pane and such commodities as fans, silk handkerchiefs, and whatnot were displayed in the front row. Two or three bright colored kimonos also were hanging on the wall.

"I have sold my wedding kimono," she said, "but I was told that I sold it at a loss. I sold it at only 300 yen, very cheap for a kimono like that."

"These kimonos are on commission sale," she said as she pointed to the hanging kimonos. "Evacuees from cities are selling their kimono to buy food."

One of the repercussions of the coming of the troops showed itself in rising prices. Five hundred yen for a second-hand kimono! We marvelled. But it was only the beginning.

There were at least seven souvenir shops in that small town and all of them prospered. The favorite articles with the soldiers were lacquer wares, china, and kimono. And what surprised the people was the taste of the soldiers in choosing a kimono. Most of them preferred a red one or one with shockingly bright colors. A somber colored kimono of refined taste had difficulties in finding a customer. "They don't appreciate our refined taste," was the shopkeepers' unanimous opinion.

In Japan, a somber colored kimono is considered of finer taste: red is only for very young girls, and purple is very popular. Older woman wear grey, dark blue, brown or black. There is a story about a kimono contest held in the Tokugawa Era. There were many women in gay colors but a woman in black was chosen as the winner of the contest. At some distance, her kimono looked just black with no designs on it, but people who came closer were surprised to find how exquisite her kimono was. On the black texture were some small designs of flowers and pearls were inlaid on them.

As it was, shopkeepers were naturally amazed when a soldier customer came in and chose a bright red kimono for "my girl" or even for "my mother".

Another thing the soldiers liked very much to take back home was a Japanese sword. "Where can I get a Japanese sword?" was the question I was asked dozens of times. But the problem was solved when Japanese swords were given to all the men.

# CHAPTER 22

# A RED CROSS NIGHT

It was not very clearly understood in the beginning. According to Mr.Kuno, some girls of good families in the town were to attend parties sponsored by the Red Cross Society. In his mind and in ours also, Red Cross was always associated with medical care so we thought we were to serve teas and sweets to sick soldiers at the camp. That was what Mr. Kuno understood it to be. None of us knew that Red Cross was taking care of soldiers' entertainment also.

Four girls were chosen from the station office, the police station, and the town office respectively, with Miss Kato and I accompanying them as chaperon-interpreters.

We were told to gather at the police station at six o'clock. When the time came, the police station was full of gay colors to the wonder of people who happened to pass by.

I asked the police chief what we were expected to do. He didn't know anything. "Don't worry, they will take you safely home," was all he knew. After a short while, Lt. Schumann came with an army truck to carry us.

"I see you are treating us like baggage," I said to him. I realized my mistake when he seriously protested, "Oh, no. This is the truck for carrying men." He wasn't the kind of man to appreciate jokes.

"What are we supposed to do?"

"You are supposed to serve the soldiers with tea, but you will be the guests tonight. They won't let you do anything. Just sit and enjoy the evening." We all felt relieved.

Free movement being restricted, the girls in kimono were being pulled up or pushed up onto the truck one by one, laughing and screaming.

"It isn't a very picturesque sight," I said to myself and went round to the front to get my seat by the driver before I was caught and tossed on to the truck.

When we started, there was still enough light to discern who was in the truck. A stream of soldiers walking toward the town saw us and called out, "Geisha girls, geisha girls!" Apparently, they took all the kimono-clad girls for "Geisha girls."

It was the first time for me, visiting the camp. Lighted buildings surrounding the ground were quiet and beautiful in the dusk. The truck pulled up at one of the buildings. It was a big hall brightly decorated with red-and-white striped curtains, colorful Japanese lanterns, and artificial cherry-blossoms. Many soldiers popped their heads out of the windows and said, "Geisha girls! Geisha girls!"

"No, we are not 'geisha girls.'" I had to make a stern face before becoming friendly and amiable.

A man came out to meet us. He said he was Sgt. Simmons, in charge of the Red Cross program. By the way, let me confess here that I could never tell a corporal from a sergeant. PFCs, I could tell, because of the simpleness of their stripe. But when another stripe is added, I do not know whether it is a corporal or a sergeant. At any rate, Sergeant Simmons affably offered us seats telling us to wait a little until more soldiers came.

We occupied one of the long wooden tables. Soldiers at nearby tables came to join us with coffee cups and cookies. Meantime, more and more soldiers were coming in by twos and threes until all the long wooden tables were occupied by them.

"This is a party exclusively for soldiers," Sgt. Simmons told us when he had asked the names of the girls. "No officer is allowed to come in here."

There was a platform at the end of the hall with a microphone standing on it. Sgt. Simmons led us on to the platform, and then, turning to me, asked me to introduce the girls to the men. He couldn't pronounce the Japanese names correctly, he said.

I was embarrassed because I did not know all the girls. "Oh, well, they wouldn't know if I made a mistake." I had the girls stand in a line and had each one step forward when I introduced her. Then, Sgt. Simmons invited the soldiers to come up and take the ladies to their tables. With a shout of joy, they dashed to the platform and snatched the girls away to their tables.

Sgt. Simmons took me to his table where there were four or five soldiers sitting. Girls in red kimono scattered about among the khaki uniforms were like flowers. The big hall was full of talking voices and laughter. Miss Kato was kindly walking from one table to another answering the boys' question and telling the girls to make themselves at home.

The girls were conversing with the soldiers with their small vocabulary of English assisted by that international language—gestures and smiles. Soldiers had thought they were fifteen or sixteen and were surprised to know that most of them were about twenty years of age.

"You are the one who speaks English?"

Two soldiers came and joined us. Then another and again two more. Finally my table was crowded with them, every one of them taking out a handkerchief, a piece of paper, a fan, or a flag to get my autograph.

"You are very popular," Sgt. Simmons remarked. I felt like a movie star!

After a while Sgt. Simmons walked up to the microphone and called to the boys with "Let's sing songs for our guests!" The soldiers responded with cheers. Some boys at a table near the door noisily stood up, went out and came back shortly afterwards with a piano. When a number of songs were sung beginning with "Let me call you sweetheart…", a boy's name was called and he was requested to play the piano. Then another boy sitting at my table was called and he sang songs in his rich tenor. Another played a harmonica and some others danced. Mr. Tiezin, the radio man, who had joined my table did a pantomime imitating a girl dressing up in the morning. It was so good that the hall resounded with laughter.

Sgt. Simmons came to me and asked if the ladies would like to dance. I went to them. Yes, they would like to learn how to dance.

"May I have the honor of dancing with you?" Sgt. Simmons said with a gallant gesture.

"But I can't," I protested.

"But unless you take the lead, the girls won't start."

"All right." I stood up.

It was the first time for them, dancing. Naturally, most of them were very clumsy partners. And their Japanese slippers added to their difficulty by slipping off whenever they took a backward step. However, both soldiers and the girls enjoyed it very much.

"I didn't know you were here. We have just been to Mr. Kuno's."

Just as we were getting ready to leave after a pleasant three hours, Ohara-san and Makino-san came in.

"Sunday. Two o'clock. At the police station."

"May I come to your home?"

Soldiers were making dates with the girls, who looked happy with flushed cheeks. They had never in their life been so enthusiastically welcomed and so kindly entertained by such a number of boys.

"*Sayonara*!" "Good night!"

"Come back again!"

We got on the several jeeps ready to take us home and drove back through the beautiful moon-lit night.

# CHAPTER 23

## WORRIED PARENTS

The next morning I asked the girls how they enjoyed the evening. Sure, they enjoyed themselves immensely. It was just like being in a dream.

However, one of the girls began, "As I got home late yesterday evening, my parents were much worried about me."

Other girls joined in and told me that their parents too were not very pleased with their daughters being in the camp. They were not worried about the girls themselves. They knew no harm was done to their beloved daughters, but what made them concerned was the gossip of the townspeople. All the girls were of marriageable age and as they were not likely to have a love marriage, their reputation in the town was very important for them in getting good spouses.

In Japan, most marriages are arranged by a "go-between". A "go-between" usually is a married couple who know both parties. Suppose there are parents who have a daughter of marriageable age. They have some pictures taken of the daughter and give them to their relatives and close family friends asking them to find a good husband for their daughter. If a friend of theirs knows a young man who is contemplating taking a wife, he will show the picture of the girl to the man and ask if he would like to meet her. The girl's curriculum vitae is usually attached to the picture, with a detailed account of her family and her personal taste and hobbies.

If the young man consents to having an interview with the girl, his picture will be sent to her parents, who will show it to the girl. But very often the man's picture is not sent to the girl's family, because a man's appearance doesn't count much and also because it is very seldom that a girl rejects a man's proposal to have an interview. Girls have always been on the passive side. Of course, if a girl has many offers of that kind, she can choose one and refuses the others, or meet the men one by one.

When both parties agree, the go-between sets the date of the interview. It is usually held at the girl's home or in a theater or a restaurant. The go-between, the man—sometimes accompanied by his family member—and the girl—always accompanied by her anxious mother who sees to it that her daughter looks her best—meet and have a dinner together, meantime keenly studying the other party.

On the following day, both parties concerned will go to the go-between to tell him what they thought of the man or the girl. If both of them are willing to go ahead with the affair, they will meet for a second time to begin the getting-to-know-each-other period for the man and the girl. Generally, it is from one month to a year. It depends on domestic conditions—if a parent is ill, the wedding naturally will be postponed—and whether the parents believe in superstitions or not. For instance, nineteen and twenty-two are bad for girls. If they get married when they are nineteen or twenty-two years old, they will have ill luck, and so it is better for them to postpone until the next year. Then presents will be exchanged between the two families and the wedding will be arranged. It is customarily performed at a shrine by a Shinto priest.

So, a girl's reputation is very important. Sometimes, the young man's family will send someone to ask about the girl at her neighboring houses. If neighbors should talk about her as "She used to go with American soldiers," it might spoil her future happiness. It was quite natural that the girls' parents were not very happy about their daughters going to the camp. I could not blame them.

Later in the afternoon, the fatherly-looking Lt. Marlor came, and among other things asked me about the previous evening. He listened to me with nods and smiles, but, when I told him how their parents felt about it, he looked seriously concerned.

"I see," he said. "I'll talk it over with my friends."

After that, the conservative parents of the girls were relieved to know that their daughters were not asked to come to the camp any more, but I am sure the girls were a bit disappointed.

# Chapter 24

# AN ACCIDENT

I received a letter from Mr. Tsuda, the custodian at the lake at Tennoji, asking me and Lt. Garden to come down and enjoy a day at the lake. Before I delivered the message to Lt. Garden, I asked my husband if I might go. If we were to make the trip, it would necessarily be on a Sunday since it was not an official trip, and I did not feel like leaving home on Sundays. He gave his consent and also gave me an assignment. Food rationing at that time was not delayed, but it consisted mostly of beans. "Again beans!" Ken-chan complained. But it was very hard to buy rice from a farmer. He wouldn't sell it to people whom he did not know because it was a blackmarket deal. So, it was to obtain rice through Mr. Tsuda's kind offices that my husband sent me.

When we arrived at Mr. Tsuda's around noon, he and his seventeen-year-old son were anxiously waiting for us. A boat was ready with some Japanese food and beer. Lt. Garden provided some American food, and five of us got in the Japanese-type small boat—Lt. Garden, the driver, Mr. Tsuda with his son, and myself. The boat was rowed by a young man standing at the stern. The two Americans found it curious and interesting.

It was a beautiful day with the mild late-October sun shining brightly above. The lake was quite a large one. It took more than two hours to go around it. In the middle part of the lake was a small shallow or two on which reed was thickly growing.

"We cut the reed, dry it and thatch the roof with it," Mr. Tsuda explained.

When we went around the shallow we saw several baskets floating on the water.

"They are fish-preserves. Let's have a look into it."

Mr. Tsuda had his son open the lid of one of the baskets.

"Not much," he said.

We all looked in turn. There were some hundreds of small carp, busily swimming in the water. They were cute little fish.

Mr. Tsuda had opened his boxes and we were enjoying various dishes of fresh vegetables and fish. Mr. Tsuda picked up a piece of *tempura* (fried fish) with his chopsticks, saying "This is it. This is the *tempura* of the carp we have just seen." It tasted good.

We went across the lake and came to the mouth of a river. We were amazed to see the water coming up instead of going down into the river.

"This lake is below sea-level. Therefore, when the tide is up, water flows in the opposite direction," Mr. Tsuda explained to us.

On the shore was a small fisherman's house, and there also was a basket or two tied to the pole on the bank. There were many crabs in the baskets, and some of them were quite large. Mr. Tsuda put some into a net bag and said, "Please take this bag with you. These crabs have an excellent taste." Quite unconscious of their fate, the crabs were moving about grotesquely in the bag. I felt sorry for them.

It was already three o'clock and we thought we had better hurry back. The sunshine had a tint of evening hue in it and made the color of the water look more blue and deep. Upon the water was the reflection of white clouds. Beyond the bank of the lake was a stretch of yellowish-green reed. No other boat was seen on this quiet lake. Our boat glided on smoothly, and we sat silent enjoying the landscape.

"Look!" said Mr. Tsuda suddenly pointing to the sky above the far end of the lake. Some wild ducks had just flown up.

"There are some more on the water."

Yes, there were hundreds of black spots turned into winged birds flying up in the sky.

"Oh, wild ducks, wild ducks!" Lt. Garden was excited.

"I have been longing to go duck hunting."

When Mr. Tsuda was told that the lieutenant was a good hunter, he suggested, "Why don't you come back with your gun next time?"

"Can I? I have a couple of friends who also love hunting. They will be delighted to join us."

I declined the invitation. Those pretty wild ducks with feathers smeared with blood and their long necks hanging lifeless—I didn't like the idea of it.

It was later than we expected when we finally got back to the shore. Mr. Tsuda told us to come in and have a cool drink, but we had not enough time for that. We thanked him and got into the jeep, where a bagful of potatoes awaited me.

"I'll send you a note when I get hold of rice," he said to me.

Then a net bag with crawling crabs was loaded, and two bottles of *sake* for thirsty Americans.

"I'll see you again Sunday next," Lt. Garden said.

"Thank you for the most enjoyable afternoon. I shall never forget this nineteenth birthday of mine," the young driver, who had remained mostly quiet during the afternoon, said to Mr. Tsuda as they shook hands.

We were driving at a good speed along the bank of a river that led us to the town of Gosen. A group of children playing on the road saw our jeep coming, and stood in lines on both sides, waving their hands to us, shouting "Hello! Goodbye!" We almost drove past them, when a small boy on the left side suddenly started running to cross the road.

"Oh!" I held my breath. Before we knew what happened, the boy fell on the grass.

"Stop!"

Lt. Garden had the jeep stopped and jumped out. I followed and went back to the boy fearing he was dead. Thank God, he was not dead. He lay motionless there, so shocked that he was not even crying. None of his limbs was severed as I had feared might be. With a sigh of relief I tried to hold him in my arms. The boy made a short cry of pain. Lt. Garden told me to lay him down and examined his body. His head, arms, chest, abdomen. No harm was done.

"Oh, here it is," Lt. Garden said. The boy shrieked. His right leg was fractured.

"We must take him to a hospital." Lt. Garden was standing up. The other children were anxiously looking at the prostrate boy.

"Where is his home? Will you go and tell his mother to come here?" I said to them.

They looked up at me without saying anything, and then all turned and looked in one direction. I followed their gaze. Down the bank were several farm houses half hidden among the trees. The door of a house was opened and against the lighted interior, we saw the figure of an old woman come running toward us. Apparently one of the children had already run down to tell her what happened.

It seemed a long time before she climbed up the bank and reached us.

"Take! Take!" she cried in tears. "Poor boy! Why did you do such a thing? I have told you a hundred times not to run across the road when a jeep comes. Why did you do it?"

"Don't be so excited. It's only a simple fracture of the leg. He'll be all right soon. Yes, he was really lucky. He might have been killed." I soothed her, and she stopped crying and bowed to the lieutenant.

"We must take him to the hospital, though. Can his mother or father come with us?"

The old woman told us that both of them were still working in the fields.

"I don't know how to apologize to them as the boy was left in my care. I should never have let him come out with older children. He is only five, and doesn't know what danger is." She again started crying.

I picked up some pieces of wood and with the lieutenant's help, gave first aid to the boy's fractured leg. I was glad I had taken the course in first aid during the war.

When it was over, Lt. Garden told the grandmother to get on the jeep. I sat by her and supported the boy's legs while the grandmother held him tight in her arms. She was talking to him in a tearful voice.

"Poor boy! Poor boy! Have patience. You'll be all right soon."

We drove back to Gosen at a cautious speed so that the movements of the vehicle did not give unnecessary pain to the boy.

I asked the lieutenant to stop the jeep at Mr. Kuno's before going to the camp. I ran in and explained the situation to Mrs. Kuno. I felt so relieved to see my boy safe in the Kuno girls' care.

"I might be delayed tonight," I told my husband hurriedly explaining what had happened and again got in the jeep. It was already getting dark but there was still some light on the summits of the mountains standing clearly against the pale blue sky. However, I was not in the mood to enjoy beautiful nature.

"Hurry up! Hurry up! Hurry up!" I kept saying to myself.

At long last, the jeep passed through the gate of the camp and stopped in front of a building. Lt. Garden jumped down and ran upstairs. One, two, three, four, five minutes.... He came out with a disappointed look.

"To the town hospital," saying to the driver, he sat down. We rushed back to the town hospital near the Muramatsu station. A surprised nurse came out at the sound of the jeep. When I explained, she told us to take the boy in and to wait a while. The doctor on duty was visiting his patient in the village.

"The doctor may come back at any time," she told us.

"At any time...." It might be midnight. I knew those doctors in rural districts—they go to visit their patients, where they are served with tea or *sake* and spend sometime chatting with the family.

"Let's go and get him," I said to Lt. Garden.

"But do you know the way?"

"We'll take the nurse along."

Again we got into the jeep.

"Watch out for a man on a bicycle. We might meet him on the way."

After driving some twenty minutes along the dark country road, we finally found the house.

As I had suspected, the doctor was drinking *sake* at the fireside. The farmer was surprised at an untimely visit of an American officer, but when he heard the story he cordially invited us to come in and have a drink.

"No, thank you. We must take the doctor back as soon as possible."

The doctor seemed rather reluctant to leave the comfortable fireside. While he was getting ready, the hospitable farmer came out again with cups of *sake* on a tray. Lt. Garden did not hesitate to take it.

"Thank you kindly." I took it and came out to give it to the driver. Poor boy! What a birthday!

We tied the doctor's bicycle to the front of the jeep, and came back through the chilly moonless night.

The doctor found it nothing very serious, but due to some reason or other which I have forgotten now, the town hospital could not give him the required treatment. He suggested a specialist in Niitsu, a big town some twenty miles away.

When I realized there was a man in working clothes at the boy's side, he was the boy's father. He bowed to us politely and said, "Please excuse me for these dirty clothes. But I was so anxious. I came out here as soon as I heard about it. I am very sorry that my boy caused you all this trouble. His name is Takeshi, and he is my fourth son."

The boy was a brave child. He lay silent with his eyes wide open. The fractured leg must have given him much pain, but he neither cried nor complained. We all felt all the more sorry for him.

As if being reminded by something, Lt. Garden looked at his watch. It was past eight o'clock.

"We must have something to eat. Come along," he said to me and the farmer.

For the second time in the course of an evening, I passed through the camp gate. Lt. Garden took us to the officers' mess hall, while the driver went to have his own supper.

There was nobody else eating in the hall and we occupied a table nearest to the kitchen. Steaming stewed vegetable and thick slices of bread with butter and jam were served. I ate with good appetite.

"Would you like some more coffee?" A mess boy came to pour into my cup for the fourth time.

"No more, thank you," I was really full.

The farmer also enjoyed the American food heartily. He had two servings of stew and remarked that he had never had such a delicious meal. It was not surprising because Japanese farmers' diets usually consists of rice, bean soup, and some pickles. They eat much but don't pay attention to introducing novel dishes. Even before the war, when we city people enjoyed all kinds of foods—Japanese, Chinese, Italian, American, German, French and Indian—these farmers were eating the same things as their great-great-great-grandfathers. They were satisfied if their stomach was full of rice.

Behind the serving counter, they were baking muffins for an officers' party.

"A special treat for you," said one of the soldiers, bringing me hot muffins just out of the oven.

"This is just the thing for the boy. We must take back some to him and his grandmother," I said to Lt. Garden. He had some more muffins wrapped up in paper and with stew in a pan, we set out again to the hospital. Lt. Garden had also brought two Japanese army blankets from somewhere and gave one to me as it was getting rather chilly.

It was a long trip to the hospital in Niitsu, and when we got there the hospital was already closed and everybody was asleep. We went round to the back door and banged. After a short while, a man in night gown appeared. He was not in good humor. It was obvious he was enjoying a pleasant sleep after some cups of *sake*, but, when he saw the American officer, he became fully awake. He told us to wait a while and went in to change.

We carried the boy, wrapped up in a blanket, to the consultation room. The doctor examined him expertly and turned to us anxious onlookers.

"He was very lucky not to have been hurt more seriously. Two weeks' stay in hospital and then after a month or so of staying in, he will be able to go out again."

We all felt relieved. The boy's father and grandmother thanked the lieutenant again and again for his kindness.

"It was entirely my boy's fault. We could not have done anything about it, if this officer had run him over and just gone ahead without stopping," the farmer said to me.

"How much does he charge for it?" Lt. Garden asked me.

"About a hundred yen including everything," was the answer.

Lt. Garden took out his pocketbook and put a hundred-yen note on the table.

"But, it was not your fault," I said.

"I know. But I feel very sorry for this boy. I too have a child at home."

The farmer did not know how to express his gratitude.

"The trouble is that plaster of Paris is hard to get these days. I wonder if the lieutenant could give us some plaster of Paris," said the doctor.

"Sure. But how shall I deliver it?"

It was decided that the boy's father was to come and get it from me at the station.

Everything being fixed, we left the hospital, leaving the grateful people behind. Now it was already cold and after hours of tension and excitement I was feeling exhausted. I sat silent between Lt. Garden and the driver looking into the darkness being cut open by the headlights.

"What are you thinking of?" Lt. Garden asked. Just at that moment, a stray hen was caught almost under the wheels when crossing our way.

"Oh!" I jumped up with a shriek.

Both the lieutenant and the driver looked at me concernedly.

"You are nervous," they said. I was thinking of my boy and of the poor child whom we had just left.

The next morning, Lt. Garden came up to the station with two packages of plaster of Paris and some bandages.

"I got the devil yesterday. I was duty officer yesterday evening, and I didn't come back in time, you know. Secondly, I was not supposed to take you on a cross-country ride. But I don't care because I had a swell time with you, although the best part of it was spoiled by that accident," he said.

# Chapter 25

# THE RAINS CAME

I had heard that Niigata was a rainy place, but I did not know that it rained so much.

It drizzled through days and days. The day dawned and closed in rain. Washed garments did not dry up for days, and the air itself was thick with moisture. Every morning I awoke discouraged by the surrounding greyness. It was very depressing and I missed the blue sky terribly.

The town was full of soldiers wearing rain coats and ponchos. *Poncho*, I liked very much. The word itself sounded funny, and, when I was told it could be made into a tent, I took a fancy to it. A soldier's head rising above an olive-colored mole was a delightful picture. I called it "smuggling coat." For they produced everything from under the poncho. Nobody would notice it if Lt. Grotious smuggled four bottles of *budoshu* into the camp, carrying them under his poncho.

"I think it's a very good idea to have holes in your poncho around the neck. If you are caught in the act of smuggling, you can hang yourself on the spot," I said to him.

However, I could not help noticing the influence of the rain on people, especially on the soldiers. I myself felt restless and irritated over trifles.

One rainy afternoon, there was a telephone call from the RTO at Niigata station. I went to call Johnson in his room. Lt. Grotious was there sitting on the cot. I was about to come back with Johnson, when Grotious-san said, "Why do you run? Stay!"

I obediently stayed at the threshold. There was something different about him. When I came in, he only said "Hello!" languidly and his face was not lit with a bright smile as usual.

He was silent for a while. Neither did I say anything. Finally he began.

"I have a faraway look in my eyes today."

"Are you homesick?"

"Terribly. I miss American women. Tall blond women in skirts. Not in baggy pants like yours."

I could not laugh. He was again gazing preoccupiedly into space where he was seeing something I could not see.

"But you will see them soon when you go to Tokyo," I said.

"You mean WACs?"

"Yes."

"They are no good. They aren't women. I hate to look at them."

"When will you be able to go home?"

"Next spring. A long time yet."

I had never seen Lt. Grotious in such a mood. Although I felt sympathetic, I knew nothing could be done to recover his usual cheerfulness. Only time and maybe sunshine would work.

"Goodbye, Melancholy Grotious. I hope you'll be Lt. Ferocious Grotious again next time I see you."

I slipped out of the room, feeling melancholy myself.

## Chapter 26

# TEACHING JAPANESE

Capt. Mattison came to see me one day. I had met him before at the mayor's party. He was a nice elderly officer.

"I heard from Lt. Garden that you have had some teaching experience," he said.

"Yes. Before the war started, I was teaching Japanese at the International Student Institute in Tokyo. It was only for a year, though. And I didn't have a big class. Just a few students."

"We have an Army school at the camp. And as some boys are interested in learning Japanese, we are planning to open a course in Japanese. Would you like to teach them? I assure you they will behave all right."

"I would be interested in teaching them. But please ask Mr. Kuno whether he is willing to let me do it, because I am employed by his company."

Both Mr. Machida and Mr. Kuno were nice enough to let me take it.

"But not every day," Mr. Kuno said.

So it was arranged that a jeep would be sent to the station at 12:45 pm on Monday, Wednesday, and Friday to take me to the camp to teach two classes.

It was during the first week of November. The next day, a very good-looking boy came up at 12:40 pm and asked for Mrs. Goto. It was my driver, who looked surprised to find me just a young girl.

"Are you ready to come?" he asked.

"Just a minute. I'll get my dictionary." I went back to my desk and stayed there for a few seconds to summon enough courage before facing my soldier-students.

This was the first time I had ever come to the camp during the daytime. In the spacious ground surrounded by many buildings, some boys were playing football. Some others were leisurely walking around. They all looked at me curiously. I sat stiff, trying to look like a dignified teacher.

The school building was situated in a corner of the compound. When we approached, I saw a tall soldier standing at the door. He waved his hand to me. It was Lt. Garden. I felt glad to find an old friend when I was feeling so tense.

"I was waiting for you. I'd like to join your class, but I have a class to teach. When it's over I'll come round to see how the boys are behaving."

He led me into a room and introduced me to a Lt. Hummel. He was a very tall intellectual-looking officer. He was even a few inches taller than Lt. Garden. I had never seen such a tall man, and, as I was measuring him in silent surprise, Lt. Garden laughingly told me that Lt. Hummel was the tallest officer in the regiment. He was in charge of the school.

After a short while, the bell rang and with it my heart started throbbing.

"I shall introduce you to the boys," Lt. Hummel led the way and Lt. Garden and I followed. The room was upstairs. There were many soldiers in the hall. They all looked surprised to see a small Japanese girl in the army school.

When the lieutenant opened the door, the talking voices inside were hushed and I found some twenty soldiers all looking at me. In the front row was a familiar face smiling. It was Ohara-san. I smiled back, feeling so very much relieved.

When Lt. Hummel introduced me to the boys, Lt. Garden

whispered, "I'll be in the next room. So, don't worry," and they both went out.

I was glad that there was no platform for the teacher. I hated to stand on the platform while teaching. But the blackboard was a little too high for me. I had to stand on my toes.

"*Kon-nichi-wa*" (Good day, or How do you do)
"*Ohayo gozaimasu*" (Good morning)
"*Ikaga desuka*" (How are you?)
"*Sayonara*" (Goodbye)
"*Domo arigato*" (Thank you)

I started with the greetings used in everyday conversation. The boys were very eager to learn. I made them say the phrases all together and then one by one speaking in Japanese as much as possible. Black-haired, Spanish-speaking boys were generally good at pronunciation but they were rather slow in grasping the meaning. When I made them repeat the same thing again and again, they did so good-naturedly grinning.

There was a very bright Jewish boy, whose understanding and pronunciation were exceedingly good. He and Ohara-san became my favourite students.

The time flew fast and soon the bell rang, telling the end of the first hour.

"*Sayonara*," I said to them.

"*Sayonara*," they responded with a satisfied look.

Ohara-san came up to me.

"I am very glad you are going to teach us. I have been wondering who the teacher was going to be," he said.

In the next class were some officers including Lt. Power and Lt. Kontz. Lt. Kontz was the new MP chief. He was a big jovial man and was as fat as a beer barrel. I wasn't surprised to learn that he had worked in a brewery before.

This class was easier to teach because the officers took the initiative and asked me many question.

As the days passed I came to enjoy teaching more and more. Some boys who had joined the class out of mere curiosity had dropped out, and the two classes grew smaller and better.

I explained to them how Japanese sentences are constructed so that they could make sentences by themselves with the aid of a dictionary. This method worked well with a few bright students. Ohara-san, who studied hard by himself, made remarkable progress. By the time I met him again in Tokyo in the following January, he was able to make himself understood in Japanese. I felt very proud of him.

Officers were much fun. They kind of disregarded their fellow soldier-students and talked to one another in Japanese or stood up and read a sentence whenever they could make one. Although I noticed that common soldiers did not like their arrogant attitude, their voluntary talking was of much help in such an informal class. I had neither textbooks nor reference books to depend on. Whenever I ran out of topics to talk about, I encouraged my students to ask questions.

One day, Lt. Power raised his hand and said that he had prepared a few sentences that he would like to read aloud.

*"Dozo yonde kudasai,"* (please read) I said.

He stood up and read a few sentences. They were about me, but I could not help laughing out loud at his *"anata wa oishii desu"* (you taste good).

Sentimental Lt. Power was hurt. He said he had spent the whole evening writing out the sentences.

"But you are not going to eat me. *Oishii* is one translation for the word *sweet* but it means tasty and cannot be applied to a person."

Then they began asking me what the Japanese words for "charming", "pretty", "beautiful", "attractive" and so on were. Apparently they wanted to use them on their girlfriends. Explaining, I realized that we Japanese have only a poor vocabulary when it comes to adjectives used for describing people. It must be due to our reserve in expressing ourselves. Maybe it is due to a lack of individuality.

They asked me among other things what the Japanese words for "sweetheart" or "honey" were. *Koibito* is one word for it, but we don't use it as Americans do. We may use it in a letter or in referring to someone, but usually we don't call to our girls "Hello, *Koibito*!" We are too serious compared with American light-heartedness, which is due, to a large extent, to the influence of Confucianism and Buddhism.

They were much interested in learning that Japanese have a number of words for just "You" and "I". Starting with *anata* and *watakushi* there are more than ten sets of "you"s and "I"s. Girls use different words from boys, and we use politer forms when we are speaking to people older or higher in social positions than ourselves. Noticing their obvious discouragement, I assured them that *watakushi* and *anata* are the words that could be used any time and any place.

Especially difficult was the use of what are called post-positions—particles that link words together. It almost seemed there were no fixed rules in their use.

However, my students began to talk in Japanese somehow or other at the end of one month, and they found it of much help when going out shopping or dating their Japanese friends. Here I must say one thing for the girls of Muramatsu. They never went out with soldiers. Perhaps they were afraid of gossip or perhaps it was because there was no place to go, but in any case they did not disappoint the boys of the town by going out with American soldiers.

## Chapter 27

# A PICNIC

It was an unusually beautiful day. White feathery clouds were floating in the blue sky, and the sun was shining brightly, inviting us to come out into the open. No one felt like sitting in the office. Mr. Kuno suggested that the girls go out for a picnic, because in a few weeks the snow would come and shut us in.

"Let's go!" We all felt very happy.

"Perhaps we can find some chestnuts."

So we set out, seven of us girls.

As we went along the street, we saw women of the town busily working in anticipation of the approaching cold. Some had taken out their warm clothes and had hung them on rope to shake off the dampness after the rains. Some were washing in the stream. By the way, this was what surprised the Americans: people of the town used the water of the river for all purposes. You could see women washing mud off vegetables while another woman a hundred yards upstream was washing diapers.

"Have they got no idea about sanitation?" the Americans wondered.

In front of the houses there were many kinds of vegetables spread on rough straw mats to dry. They were getting ready for the five long months when they had to live in snow. Red persimmons were hanging under the eaves of every house. When they get dry, they are very sweet and have exquisite flavor.

In order to go to a small hill where some chestnut trees grow, we had to pass the barracks and the parade ground which was at the back of the barracks. As we came toward it, a jeep came from the opposite direction. Sgt. Nishi was on it. He noticed us and stopped the jeep.

"I'm leaving for home tomorrow," he said and shook hands with us.

"*Gokigenyo!*" (Farewell)

"*Sayonara!*"

Looking after his jeep, one of the girls began.

"I heard that he fell in love with a geisha girl in Sanjo and paid 10,000 yen to set her free. It was very nice of him."

It is commonly believed that Japanese "sell" their daughters as geisha girls. It is not exactly selling. When poor parents are really in need, they sometimes borrow money from the operator of a geisha house in exchange for the service of their daughter—usually about fifteen years of age. And the girl works as a maid at the same time receiving training in a geisha girl's accomplishments—music, dancing, and so on. And when she grows old enough to be a geisha girl, she starts paying off her employer. However, it very often happens that the amount of money borrowed by her parents has so increased with accumulating interest that she is never able to pay it off—especially when she herself has to borrow money to make her kimonos—until she finds a rich patron who pays a ransom and takes her as his mistress or wife. A geisha girl set free by an American soldier was quite symbolic. The dawn of happy days for the long-enslaved women of Japan!

"*Kon-nichi-wa!*" (Good day!)

"*Kon-nichi-wa!*"

We exchanged greetings with the guard standing at the entrance to the parading ground and walked on.

When we came a little way on the hill, we saw a group of American soldiers repairing the road. As we approached, they all stopped working and called to us.

"Hello!"

"Where are you going?"

We came to the top of the hill and took our lunch. The view was open, and we could look down upon the neighboring villages where smoke was coming up from the farm houses scattered around in the fields. It was peaceful. Looking down at the landscape I remembered, as if in a dream, that only three months before we were fighting desperately against the friendly soldiers whom we had just passed by.

We lay down upon the grass. It was so pleasantly warm that I began to feel drowsy.

"Hello!" Suddenly a voice said. We jumped up to find four soldiers standing a few steps away.

"Hello!" I said.

"Oh, you speak English?

I nodded.

"We saw you come up and came after you."

"We have come to gather chestnuts. But it seems we are too late."

As was usually the case with those American soldiers, they took out their pictures and showed them to me.

When they were gone, Miss Shirai asked me.

"Is it true they are going away pretty soon?"

"I don't know," I replied. "I have asked them, but no one was sure."

"We shall miss them very much. They are much fun. As my brothers have a tailor shop, they come in very often to have their clothes mended. They like to have their uniform fit them exactly. Many soldiers come to have their sleeves or pants shortened or lengthened. We enjoy their visits very much. They are so lighthearted and curious. They look into our kitchen and are surprised that we burn wood for cooking," Miss Shirai said.

"They come to my house often, too," Miss Nakamura joined in. She lived near the camp.

"Of course we cannot speak English, but nevertheless we enjoy it and manage to make ourselves understood with the help of that conversation book they carry."

"I was scared of them at first. They are so big." Little Miss Kaneko said. "I expected them to be more rough and cruel. They are really nice people."

"Mr. Kuno will be really sorry if they are to go."

He was enjoying his association with the Americans very much. He did everything he could to please and entertain them. He never let *sake* go out of stock and always served it abundantly to his American friends. What's more, he had given up his office at the station. He had his desk moved to the big room with Miss Kato as his secretary. He proposed to offer the big room also for the officers' club, but it was declined with thanks. They did not want to make noise when people were working hard downstairs.

I appreciated his efforts to entertain the Americans, but at the same time I could not help wondering how he could get hold of all the *sake* and foodstuff. My husband loved *sake* but he had not had a single drop for months although it was supposed to come through official distribution channels.

Mr. Kuno, knowing that my husband enjoyed drinking, often invited him to join the company. But my husband stubbornly declined. It was below his dignity to satisfy his desire by taking advantage of my association with American soldiers whose conversation he couldn't understand very well. But he was broad-minded enough to let me have fun with them. He knew that, whatever freedom he might give me, I was always at his rein's end

Our chat continued for a while and then we started for home singing songs that we learned from our American friends.

# CHAPTER 28

## CAPONE'S NEPHEW

---

The rumor proved to be true. The troops were moving out of the town. They were going to the Tokyo and Yokohama area. The comings and goings of soldiers became frequent, and we were kept busy all the time. The Shibata camp was folded up, and the troops hitherto staying in the city of Shibata came to join the Muramatsu camp. They were several hundred men belonging to the 3rd battalion.

They came in two trains and while they thronged at the Muramatsu station waiting for transportation, I noticed they were more rough and noisy than the soldiers staying at Muramatsu. They came into the station office, molested the girls, and some of them did not even hesitate to relieve themselves without taking the trouble of going to the restroom.

"Noisy soldiers." We frowned upon them.

"They all belong to the same regiment. I wonder why it is that the soldiers at the Muramatsu camp are much better-behaved than the soldiers from Shibata."

"Probably people of Shibata are to blame for that. Shibata is a big commercial town and the people are rough-tempered. Perhaps they did not treat the soldiers as nicely as we have done. People of Muramatsu are really nice and quiet-mannered, and it must have pacified the veterans also."

Among the Shibata soldiers was a boy of apparent Italian

origin—black hair and big black eyes. He was one of the soldiers from whom the girls ran away.

"I am Capone's nephew," he said.

"Are you really?"

When I asked dubiously, his companions assured me that he was. I studied his features carefully. His thick nose and sensual lips together with the dauntless look in his black eyes truly carried the image of his notorious uncle.

"Still love me?"

He would put his arm around a girl's neck suddenly. I was one of the victims before I knew who he was.

"I have never loved you." I snapped back and was always on my guard whenever he appeared. Other girls were very scared of him. When they saw him, they all hid themselves in safer corners. Even the ticket examiner on duty asked her male co-worker to take her place when he was around.

One day he appeared with a big adhesive tape on his nose. He said he had a row with his friends. It gave a comic note to his otherwise sinister look.

# Chapter 29

## BLACKMARKETING

It was one of those days when the whole atmosphere was disquieted by busy comings and goings. Miss Kato and I met two soldiers—truck drivers—who whispered to us asking if we wanted to buy some army sugar. Miss Kato and I exchanged a glance. Of course we coveted it, but we knew it was strictly against the law.

"But how..."

"There will be no danger at all. We can carry it out safely by the truck."

The temptation was too strong, but we could not afford to buy the whole bag by ourselves. So we told the soldiers to wait until the next day and asked Mr. Mitsuno and Mr. Kuno if they wanted to join. They jumped at the proposal and it was arranged between us that the soldiers were to take the bag to Miss Nakamura's house, whose father was a dealer in rice.

During the night set for the two soldiers to carry out the sugar bag, there was a fire at the camp. It started from the gasoline stove that they had begun to use in the camp.

The Kunos had company as usual. That night it was Johnson and Limon who were warming themselves by the charcoal stove.

Suddenly we saw a flame rise in the direction of the camp.

"Fire!"

Mr. Kuno jumped to the telephone and called the Muramatsu station. Yes, it was the camp that was on fire. Johnson came to the window to watch. But Limon-san did not even stand up. He was in love with the oldest girl, Kazuko-san, and she was more important to him.

Mr. Kuno looked at his wrist watch and then at the clock on the wall.

"Hey! I'm going to the station." He called to his wife.

"Get my clothes. Hurry up!"

He threw away his kimono, jumped into his trousers and jacket—all in front of our eyes—and off he went hurry-scurry to the station.

Johnson-san who was watching this amusedly, looked out of the window again and said.

"It seems the fire is being put out. I wonder if he is going to quench it himself. It's no use going."

I was secretly worried about the fate of my sugar.

On the following day Mr. Mitsuno and I went to the Nakamura house to get the sugar. We noticed that a corner of the bag was ripped open.

"You know that camp was on fire last night. Although it was only one building that was burnt down, there was much confusion around here. As this house is so near to the camp, people came to help us carry out our rice bags and furniture. It must have been torn open during the commotion," Mr. Nakamura explained. I was sure some sugar was stolen.

When we got back to the station, Mr. Mitsuno, a shrewd keeper of a grocery store, took his share—one fourth of the original weight—and so did Miss Kato. I was too timid to suggest that we share the loss evenly.

So I took the remaining sugar back home and gave another one fourth to Mrs. Kuno. When I weighted the rest, I realized it cost me very much. Almost one fifth of my sugar was stolen. I was much disappointed.

When I recounted the story to my husband who came back from his monthly visit to Tokyo, he laughed and said.

"It served you right. It was a heavenly warning for you never to put your hand in a blackmarket deal again."

However, I may add that he enjoyed the sweet rice-cake I prepared for him very much.

## CHAPTER 30

# SALMON FISHING

"Let's start!" said Mr. Machida as he came into the office.

"Are you ready?" Mr. Kuno asked me.

"Where are we going?" I was surprised.

"We are taking Lt. Kontz for salmon fishing. And you will come with us, of course."

I had been told nothing about it. I looked at my kimono in embarrassment. Kimono isn't a costume for going fishing. The day before, I bicycled to the rice distribution office to get my ration and fell into a ditch. As a result I could not wear my slacks and shoes—my only pair—that day.

A river went round through the town and the rice distribution office was on the road along the river. I had just learned to ride a bicycle and the rice bag was so heavy. Besides, I should have started with my right foot instead of the left ... As it was, I literally jumped into the river—fortunately it was only thigh-deep—with the bicycle and the rice and all. I barely saved the rice, which was to support us for half a month. When I came back to the station and was just about to sneak away, Lt. Marlor caught me. He stared at my miserable plight and said, "Well, Goto-san, I hope you will never try to commit suicide again." I was very glad it was not Ferocious Grotious.

"But you see, Mr. Kuno, I am in kimono today."

"That's all right. Come on."

Lt. Kontz, the stout MP chief, was waiting in his jeep.

We drove through the town of Gosen and after driving about twenty minutes along the bank of the river we made our way along a branch of river until we saw a small hut on the beach. It was a peculiar shaped hut—triangular and made of dried reed. A fisherman came out of the hut to meet us. He led us to the shore where a long shallow-bottomed boat was moored. There was another boat upstream from which a naked fisherman was keenly watching the water with a spear in hand.

Our fisherman lightly jumped into his boat followed by the slow and careful lieutenant. Then I expected Mr. Machida and Mr. Kuno to get in, but they told me to go on board.

"The boat is too small for five of us, and we know how it is," they said.

So I tucked my long sleeves inside my *obi* (sash) and carefully stepped down the cliff. Having been brought up with my brothers and used to playing ball instead of dolls, I made it easily, in spite of my bothersome kimono. I sat at the stern with the lieutenant in the center.

The boat glided upstream toward the other boat. The water was clear and we could almost see the bottom though the green water. The river was about ten meters wide, and the late afternoon sunrays falling through leaves overhead were dancing on the water.

"If it were earlier, we could see better because there would be no shade on the surface of the water."

So saying, the boatman handed a box-like square thing to Lt. Kontz, and told him by gesture to look into the water. The box had a glass bottom.

"Oh, this is wonderful!" the lieutenant exclaimed.

When I looked into the river through the glass, I could see everything very clearly. In the shade of the rocks at the bottom and through the streaming weeds, I could discern the shape of passing fish.

"See a salmon?" the boatman asked. With a disappointed "No", I handed the glass back.

"It swims very fast and is always hiding," the boatman said and shouted, "Caught any?" to the man in the other boat, who in response shook his head.

Then, the other fisherman rowed his boat still upstream and to the opposite shore which was a sandy shallow, and stripped off his pants and became stark naked. While I was wondering what he was going to do, he walked slowly into the water.

"Gee! He must be cold!" It was already nearing the end of November.

He went knee-deep, thigh-deep and then, with a splash, dived into the water. I strained my eyes against the sun to find his figure, but after a short while his head appeared at quite an unexpected place. He took a long breath and again disappeared. After a few dives in vain, he finally came up with a big salmon under his arm. We clapped our hands in applause.

The salmon was about three feet long and on its side was a cut made by the spear. It was still alive.

When we came back to the shore, we were invited into the hut. At the entrance a rough straw mat was hung by way of a curtain and inside was a small room that accommodated only six or seven people.

Around the fire we sat on the straw mats each with a plate, bowl, cup and chopsticks. Above the fire was hung a large pot from the top of the triangle-shaped ceiling. An appetite-stimulating smell of cooking salmon, horse-radish, and onion filled the interior. The fisherman came in with slices of salmon stuck on tongs and put them in the ash around the fire. On the wall were hung various fishing tackle and fishermen's clothes.

While I was looking around with curiosity, the fisherman took the lid of the pot off and served us its contents. Salmon and vegetables were cooked in Japanese sauce. It was steaming hot, and so delicious and fresh! The two American guests, Lt. Kontz and his driver, sitting tightly in the tiny room did not decline whenever the toastmaster, the fisherman, offered them another bowl of stewed salmon and vegetables.

"I have never eaten such a tasty fish," they said again and again. Lt. Kontz who was one of my pupils in Japanese was thinking hard to express himself in the newly-learned language. Their Japanese hosts, Mr. Machida and Mr. Kuno, watched their American guests devour the meal with cups of *sake* and a look of satisfaction.

Although I held it against Mr. Kuno that he had a mistress and was proud of it, I couldn't dislike him when I saw him generously smiling with his narrow eyes hidden between the wrinkles.

At last we were really full. Lt. Kontz put down his chopsticks for good with a sigh of contentment and "*Mo takusan desu*" (no more, thank you).

When I came out into the fresh open air from the closeness of the interior thick with the smell of *sake* and food, I felt good and I breathed in the cool serenity of the November evening. The driver and I joined Lt. Kontz in thanking Mr. Kuno and Mr. Machida for the unexpected party.

On our way back, jovial Lt. Kontz who was in particularly good humor after cups of *sake* suddenly turned back and asked "Do Japanese people kiss?" I translated the query for Mr. Machida and Mr. Kuno and then answered, "There is a historic document of the sixteenth century in which the writer of the letter, a famous warlord, mentioned kissing his mistress. So I don't think it is a new custom introduced by the Westerners. And whether contemporary Japanese kiss or not, you will get the answer from Mr. Machida and Mr. Kuno's faces."

Lt. Kontz looked at their grinning faces and laughed aloud.

When the jeep pulled up at the station entrance, I stood up to jump down as usual. But being in kimono I was not alert enough: the big Lt. Kontz picked me up in his arms and lightly put me down on the ground in the midst of all the curious-eyed middle school boys waiting for their train. It was so embarrassing. I felt I would surely lose their respect.

"Don't! This is not a Japanese custom." My protest was too late.

"You should have told me so before."

The Americans laughed and drove away around the corner.

# CHAPTER 31

## THE FIRST SNOWFALL

With the arrival of December, the cold snowy winter came. Since the beginning of November we had seen little of the blue sky. The sky was grey and low all the time. On the night of the first of December it started to snow heavily. When I looked out of the window the next morning, the entire world was clad in silvery snow with the black trains at the station yard looking all the more black against the whiteness of the snow.

When I reached my office, I found both Johnson and Roderiguez excited like children. Roderiguez-san who was brought up in a warm region had never seen snow before.

"This is the first snow I have ever seen in my life," he said, and running out again into the yard, he grabbed at the snow, made it into a ball and threw it as far as he could reach.

The younger workers at the station who usually gather around the stove and chat were alike excited about the first snowfall. They too ran out into the yard and began to attack Roderiguez-san and Johnson-san with snow balls. There was no team. Every one attacked the nearest person. But Johnson and Roderiguez were the main targets of all. Within a few minutes, their uniforms were all white and they were covered with snow from neck to ankles.

Miss Kato and I joined in the fight, but in a few seconds we had to run for our lives back into the office.

When we were resting by the stove watching the boys still

fighting in the smoke of the powder snow, an army truck stopped in front of the station. It was Lt. Marlor, Lt. Kopfs, and Lt. Steel who came to say "*Sayonara*" to us. They were among the first to leave Muramatsu.

Mr. Kuno, Miss Kato, and I saw them off at the front entrance of the station.

"Goodbye and good luck!"

"When are you coming back to Tokyo?" Lt. Marlor asked me.

"Maybe soon, I don't know. Oh, Lt. Marlor, please send me just one square inch of blue sky from Tokyo. I am dying for the blue sky and sunshine."

The word Tokyo brought back to me all the happy memories of my home town.

"I'll mail it in a letter to you."

The door shut on the smiling face of Lt. Marlor, and the truck soon became a tiny black dot far across the white fields.

## CHAPTER 32

## "SAYONARA!"

Some people said that the Americans were not leaving until the end of the year. No one was sure about it until at last it was definitely known that they were leaving—all of them—in the beginning of December. Some scores of men would stay two or three weeks longer under Captain Robinson for the purpose of closing up the camp, but all the rest were going away soon. Mr. Kuno was terribly disappointed.

"After all these enjoyable days I've spent with them, how shall I keep myself occupied?" he lamented.

"It makes me sad to think that I shall never again be able to smoke American cigarettes," the jolly station master of Gosen said. Mr. Machida also was sorry because he could no longer practise his long-forgotten-and-newly-recovered English on the American soldiers. Souvenir shop keepers naturally were sorry and so were some other people of the town who had cultivated a taste for American cigarettes and candies.

I asked people I met as to how they felt about the American soldiers leaving the town. None of them were too eager to see them go. They expressed their regret at their going away so soon.

"We were very surprised because they are such nice people. We were told to regard them as beastly demons during the war," they said.

"Moreover, I anticipated that they would consume all our

foodstuff leaving nothing for us to eat, but they did not take anything from us, but brought everything from America—potatoes, canned food, meat and even eggs were sent from home. It was only beer that they took from us, and that we can do without."

"What impressed me most was their friendliness toward us. They did not act like conquerors, but they treated us just like friends."

"I think we are very lucky to be occupied by the Americans. This prefecture being so close to the Soviet Union, I was afraid that the Russians might come in. They say they are terrible."

As it was, when the first group of troops left the town on trucks, the whole town was out to see them off. They lined up on both sides of the street, with children in the front row, and cheered and waved their hands.

"*Sayonara*! *Sayonara*!"

"Goodbye! Hello!"

"Goodbye! Hello!" Children shrieked at the top of their voices.

From the window of the station office we watched the trucks go by. The sky was threatening to snow again. One after another, the dark olive-colored trucks went by with olive-clad soldiers on them. All waved their hands to us. On every one of the trucks we recognized one or two of our friends.

"Here comes Limon-san!"

"Oh, that's Roderiguez-san standing up!"

"Goodbye! *Sayonara*!"

They were all gone. I felt the bleakness of the landscape all the more strongly after the excitement. I looked far out to the fields covered in grayish whiteness. I was very envious of the soldiers. For they were going to Tokyo, to Tokyo where my father was. I missed him very much. But I remembered sadly that we had no house to go back to in Tokyo.

The train for Tokyo was scheduled to leave from Gosen at one o'clock in the afternoon. So, Mr. Kuno, Miss Kato—who wore a pink dress and silk stockings for the special occasion of seeing Johnson-san off—and I were to go down to the Gosen station later.

Johnson who stayed at the camp the night before came back to the station in the morning to pack. He had almost finished his packing, but owing to his popularity with the people of the town, his baggage swelled up with many additional presents. He had to pack again. But there were some bulky presents that he could not possibly take back with him. He beckoned us to a corner and said, "This is Mr. So-and so's gift. But I cannot carry it. So I'll give this to you as my *presento*. Please don't tell him."

When he was through, he went round to shake hands with all the people of the station. Every one of them was sorry to see him go.

"I hate to go. I wish I could stay here longer," he said.

With one foot on the stepboard of the train, he turned to have a last look around. He had tears in his blue eyes. The girls began to sob. I turned aside to hide my tears. He was so much liked by all. Even my husband, who had met him only once or twice, admired him saying that Johnson really seemed a fine man in spite of the fact that he was a mere farmer. It was his sincerity that won our hearts. Indeed, he was one of the best ambassadors that America had ever sent out to a foreign country.

We accompanied him to the Gosen station, where most of the soldiers were already seated in the carriages. Many others were out on the platform sauntering about and chatting with friends. They looked very happy, for going to Tokyo meant a step nearer home.

The first carriage was reserved for Col. Payne and the officers. He had not arrived yet.

Shortly after we arrived, Mr. Kuno's daughters came and joined us. Limon-san came out of the carriage, strolled as far as the end of the platform with Kazuko-san, where they stopped and were engaged in conversation. Kazuko-san took out her handkerchief and put it to her eyes. She was crying.

Some of the soldiers were looking at them, grinning and saying something to each other. Mr. Kuno noticed it and said to his other daughters.

"Shame on her! Go and tell her to come back here."

But the younger girls would not move. They knew she was in love with Limon, and remembering her unhappy marriage, they felt sorry for their older sister.

On the next train from Muramatsu came Mr. and Mrs. Machida bringing their youngest daughter with them, who held a big bouquet of flowers in her arms.

They went into the station master's room, and, when I turned my eyes toward it, I saw Col. Payne and some other officers resting there in the room.

I made my way toward it, because I wanted to thank Col. Payne for the books he sent me as a reward for teaching Japanese. But before I reached the room, a soldier ran out from a carriage and called to me, "Goto-san!" It was Ohara-san.

"I have been looking around for you. I was afraid that I might miss you," he said. "Makino-san is leaving tonight for Sendai."

The two good friends were going to be separated because Makino-san was going to join the 11th Airborne.

"I'll see him off. I'll let you know as soon as we go back to Tokyo. If you stay in Tokyo long enough, I'm sure we can see each other again," I said.

"I'm looking forward to it," he replied. I showed him where Mr. Kuno and his daughters were, and he walked down the platform toward them.

When I joined them again, Miss Kato was not with them. I found her inside the carriage where Johnson was. Seeing that there were only a few minutes left before the train was to start, I went toward them to say the last *Sayonara* to Johnson. When I approached one of the windows, Howard and Grey leaned out of the window with outstretched hands.

"I didn't know you were here. I'm very glad to see you once again before we go," they said.

"So am I. You were the first American soldiers I ever met in my life. Do you remember the first day you came in?" I asked.

"Sure. I was really surprised and delighted to meet you."

At this moment, Col. Payne came out of the station room.

"All on board" was shouted and all the soldiers who were still out on the platform hurriedly got into the carriages. Johnson picked up Miss Kato in his arms, walked through the carriage and put her down on the platform. Then he went back to the window, took the youngest Kuno daughter Aiko's hand and kissed it.

After shaking hands with Johnson, I returned to join the Machidas and Kunos. Little Miss Machida presented her bouquet to Col. Payne just before he went into the carriage. Col. Payne expressed a few words of appreciation to the mayor and got on board.

Someone called me out of one carriage. I turned and found Lt. Butler sitting by the window. I stooped down, picked up some snow, and going to him, pressed it hard into his hand pretending to shake hands.

"You naughty girl!" Lt. Butler laughed and threw it back at me.

Suddenly a group of girls in multi-colored kimono almost tumbled down the steps to the platform. They were, I heard someone say, prostitutes of the town. They ran from window to window calling their lovers' names. Some soldiers leaned out of the windows and held them tight in their arms.

"Charlie! Charlie!"

One pretty young girl in red kimono was still running, looking into each and every window. The whistle had already blown, but her Charlie did not show his face. Perhaps he was not on the train or he was too shy to lean out of the window. The train started moving. She finally gave up and cried tearfully on her friend's shoulder.

We walked to the end of the platform with the slowly moving train. While we stood there, faces of many friends passed by. Johnson, Limon, Roderiguez, O'Hara and many others. We stood in silence and watched the train until it was gone far away toward the snow-clad mountains.

Late that evening Lt. Power left the town as the commander of a unit. Lt. Garden and Makino-san went to join the 11th Airborne.

I had to come back to the station by all means to see Lt. Grotious off. It was a cold, sleeting night. The Kunos also came to see their favorite lieutenant off.

Lt. Grotious, with his arm around Aiko-san, was joking as usual.

"Goto-san refuses to be my girl. But you are. You will come to Yokohama with me, won't you?"

"Daddy says 'No.'"

"Don't pay any attention to him. Just get in the train and elope."

However, this could not be done in secrecy since I was translating it to Mr. Kuno, who presented Grotious-san with a bottle of his cherished whisky.

When the time came for the train to leave, Lt. Grotious took my hand and for once he looked serious.

"It was good knowing you. We've had lots of fun together."

"Thank you. Whenever I see a bottle of *budoshu* I'll remember you," I replied.

When we came back to Mr. Kuno's and sat around the fire drinking hot tea served by Mrs. Kuno, we all felt lonesome.

# CHAPTER 33

## LATER DAYS

Within a few days the town of Muramatsu became desolate. When evening came, there were no more American soldiers walking down the street from the camp. Souvenir shops were nearly all closed. No more jeeps were seen. Only a truck or two were seen occasionally running to and from the station to send out the rest of the Army goods.

At the RTO office, three new boys took over, and it was turned into a truck drivers' club house. Every time the drivers came to the station they spent some time with us. We talked or sang together. The favorite song with them was a Japanese soldiers' song called "Goodbye, Rabaul." They had inserted the word "Okinawa" and later "Muramatsu" in place of Rabaul and sang it in Japanese.

One of the three boys was a big Swedish man. He was almost over-generous and was in the habit of giving away everything as *presento*—C rations, cigarettes, and when they left, they even gave us some blankets that originally belonged to the Japanese Army.

He invited Miss Kato and me to partake of the lunch that was brought for them by truck drivers. It was carried in metal utensils and was very good. The boys complained they were tired of eating the same thing every day, but it was a treat for us.

In the meantime, snow was falling thick every day, and after a heavy snowfall which stopped the trains, they started to use the rotary plough. Icicles hung two or three feet long from the eaves of houses, and all the passengers were wearing rubber boots.

In several weeks the whole town would be buried under snow which would reach the second floor. Then, the people would walk only under the roof that projected over the sidewalks of the street. In order to go to the other side, a tunnel would be made in the snow at convenient places.

The sky was grey and dark all the time. Not even a patch of blue was to be seen.

"Are we going to spend the gloomy winter in this town?" I felt miserable.

# Chapter 34

## "WHAT TIME, UENO?"

On the twenty-first of December, my husband came back from Tokyo after a few days stay there.

Before he went, he had received an offer of a position at an academic institute in Kyoto. His institute was going to be dissolved. He asked me if I would go to Kyoto.

"No," I promptly answered, "I'll be a stranger in Kyoto. I want to go back to Tokyo, to my father."

When he left, he said he was going to consult his professor at Tokyo University who recommended him to the position in Kyoto.

I could hardly wait for his return. So, without even greeting him with "Welcome home!" I asked "What's the news?" Then, he tantalizingly disclosed that he was appointed instructor at the First Higher School (now a part of Tokyo University under the new education law), a position for which many young scholars would be envious of him.

I literally jumped up with joy.

"Then we can go back to Tokyo. We can see the blue sky and my father." It did not occur to me in the midst of my excitement that we had no house in Tokyo—not even a room for our family of three since my father's house also was burnt down.

When I was reminded of that, I was so disappointed. Perhaps my Ken-chan and I had to stay here in the snow while my husband alone went back to Tokyo.

After enjoying my dejected look for a few minutes, my ill-natured husband revealed that he had found an apartment in addition. His Chinese friend was going home in a month or two and we could move into his three-room apartment when he left. Besides, my husband's mother had invited us to spend the intervening time with her. I grabbed Ken-chan's hands and danced about in the room. He too was happy when I told him we were going back to see his grandfather.

The landlady downstairs—we had moved out of Mr. Kuno's house since I was of no more use to him—came up to see what was going on.

"We are going back to Tokyo—as soon as possible," I told her. The old woman was born and spent her girlhood in Tokyo.

"Yes, it really is a nice place. Warm with fine weather." She envied me.

I started to pack at once. Then I stopped my busy hands in disappointment. Since a few days before, box-cars were not available. Their use for private purposes was forbidden. I worked my mind hard to think out a solution. I was struck with an idea. "Perhaps Captain Robinson could help me."

All the way down to the camp I prayed that he would still be at his post. Two days before we were told that he would be leaving in a few days. He might be busy visiting places.

Fortunately he was at the camp and kindly wrote me a letter authorizing me to use one of the box-cars reserved for the Army.

The following two days were extremely busy days for us. We had to pack and to visit friends both in Gosen and Muramatsu. Finally on the morning of the twenty-fourth we carried our baggage to the station and saw that they were safely locked in a box-car. However, there was still another thing that troubled us. That was the problem of how to get seats in a crowded train. Trains were awfully crowded in those days. Passengers—even women—were getting in and out of the windows. We could not do that with our hand baggage and a baby.

We decided to go down to Niigata, the terminal, and take the train from there. I was prepared to stand all the way back to Tokyo—more than twelve hours —if we were lucky enough to get into the train.

When we got off at the Niigata station, a soldier who was walking about on the platform raised his hand in recognition. He was an RTO conductor whom I had met before. My heart brightened with a ray of hope. I went up to him and explained the situation and asked if he could let us ride in a corner of the military car. Fortunately he was going back to Tokyo by the same train.

"Come to see me just before the train starts. There will be no other passengers in the carriage since a sleeper is attached," he said.

A few minutes before the train started we tried to make our way through the crowd to the military car. But it was impossible. We could not walk an inch against the stream of people rushing to the train. We thought ourselves very fortunate when we managed to get into one of the carriages that was already jammed even to the toilet.

At the next station we jumped off, ran down the platform and got to the military car, where the RTO man was anxiously waiting.

"I have been wondering what happened to you," he said and then he looked at my Ken-chen.

"What a baby! How cute he is!" Ken-chan had become quite at ease with Americans and went readily to his arms. The boy tickled him and enjoyed Ken-chan's laughs and struggles very much.

As he had said, there were no passengers in the carriage except for a young Japanese conductor and his friend. We had the carriage all to ourselves. We felt sorry for other Japanese passengers in the crowded carriages, but when the RTO man retired to his berth, we took comfortable postures for sleeping. But I was too excited to go to sleep. The sound of the wheels were echoing with the words in my mind, "To Tokyo, to Tokyo, to Tokyo …."

After about two hours, the RTO man came back. He brought some beer, peanuts, and candies with him. Although it was still midnight, it was already Christmas Day. He shared the refreshments with us in celebration of the Christmas morning. Then he went to the seat in a corner where the Japanese conductors were sound asleep. He shook him and when the young boy opened his eyes, he asked, "What time, Ueno?"

The boy blinked his eyes several times before he answered, "Six o'clock." At this, the RTO man started laughing and turning to us said, "Every time we ride in the same train, he says that the train arrives at Ueno at six. But it never does. Ten o'clock at best."

After that he kept asking him every thirty minutes, "What time Ueno?" The boy was stubborn, and every time his answer was "six o'clock.

"I'll give you a hundred yen if it arrives at six—or even by eight. A hundred yen!"

The boy knew by now that the train would be late. Yet he held fast to his "six o'clock." Both of them were apparently enjoying the game. We too became interested in it, and whenever the train stopped at a big station, we looked at the station clock and at the time table.

The train was delayed. It became clear at the promised six o'clock that we had still at least four more hours to ride before we would reach the Ueno Station, the northern entrance to the city of Tokyo. But I did not mind it at all. It had been a wonderful trip, and at any rate we were already so close to Tokyo. Besides, look! It is a lovely day, with the sky so intensely blue!

Summer, 1946